Try Faith

IRENE HORN-BROWN

ISBN 978-1-63961-060-0 (paperback)
ISBN 978-1-68570-746-0 (hardcover)
ISBN 978-1-63961-061-7 (digital)

Christian Faith Publishing, Inc.
832 Park Avenue
Meadville, PA 16335
www.christianfaithpublishing.com

Printed in the United States of America

DEDICATION

My deceased parents, John and Christine, I love you and miss you, Mom and Dad.

To my three heartbeats: Jerry Brown, Karol Brown-Shoffner, and Madeline Simpkins, I love you guys more than life itself.

To ALL of my grands, great-grands, and my unborn great-grandchildren, I love you.

Much love from your daughter, mom, ma, mammie, nannie, and mama Brown.

CONTENTS

ACKNOWLEDGMENTS

God, thank You for blessing me and making my dreams become a reality. Without You and my faith, this would not have happened.

Christian Faith Publishing, thank you for taking a chance with me and the success of my book *Try Faith*. God bless.

My three children, Jerry, Karol, and Madeline, I am so proud that you are my children. I love you.

Patricia (Pat), my sister, my friend, thank you for your prayers and support. I love you always.

Taneya, my granddaughter, who came to my rescue whenever I ran into trouble (which was often) with something concerning my laptop. Taneya supported me with her encouragement when I was feeling like giving up on my book. I love you, Taneya, for all you have done for me.

Te'Ana, my granddaughter, who has given me moral support from the first day I told her about my dream of wanting to become a successful fiction writer. Te'Ana, you and I have spent many, many mornings, evenings, and nights together talking about our dreams and our relationships with God. We have spent many times laughing, talking, eating, encouraging each other, and yes, we have also had times where we cried together. But through it all, we can truly say that God is good. Thank you, Tee, and I love you always.

My grandchildren:
Royan Brown
Anthony Wilson
Rashad Brown
Byron Shoffner II
Trequiana Simpkins
Rakeem Brown
KahBria Gonzles
Te'Ana Cintron
Raycel Brown
David Simpkins III
Taneya Simpkins
Jeremiah Brown

My great-grandchildren:
Zair Brown
Jay'Vion Brown
Myon Shoffner
Nayhani Brown
Mylon Shoffner
Emayah Brown
Royan Brown II
Gabriel Cintron
Ianeta Wilson
Javion Gonzalez

My godchildren:
Ed Davis

Tina Davis
Tyson Davis
I love you guys very much.
To ALL of my children out there, I love you dearly.

My siblings:

My big brother James Surratt (JC). Thank you for being my brother. I love you.

My sister Corene Atkins. Thank you, sis, for being my sister. I love you.

My sister Earnestine Lewis. I love you, sis. God bless you.

My sister Patricia (Pat) Atkins. Hey there, sister-friend. I am so happy you are my sister. I love you.

My sister Ella Mae. I thank you, sis, for being my friend ever since you were a little girl. You are the best. I love you.

My little brother Earl. Earl, I am scratching my head because I really don't know what to say to you other than I love you.

My sweet little baby sister Louise. Hi, sis. I am so happy that you are my little sister. You are so kind and caring. I love you.

My college professors:

Mrs. Moncia Tapiarene. Thank you so much for working so diligently with me with my English classes. (English, my worst subject.) And thank you for encouraging me to go for my dream: a successful fiction author/writer!

Mrs. Marci Sanchez. Thank you for encouraging me to pursue my dream as a successful fiction writer

Mr. William Martin, thank you so much for your encouragement, telling me that I could be that successful writer that I always dreamed of wanting to be.

Joyce Beal, my longtime and lifetime friend (aka Ms. Texas to me). Sis, we have been through a lot together in our lifetime, and I am so happy that we can say God was with us through it all. Thank you, sis, for being a great friend and sister. I love you always.

Liz Long. Hi, Liz, your friends, Joyce Beal and I, miss you so much. We know that you are looking down from heaven watching over us. (You were the one that thought logically in our group. Joyce was hotheaded and I was scary. LOL.) I love you.

Gladys Britton, my best friend. Hey, girl! Thank you for all the fun, laughs, traveling, and just good ole conversations. Friends always. I love you, sis.

Cheryl Turner, my friend, my sister in Christ. Thank you for the encouraging Bible scriptures and your encouraging words. God bless you. Love you.

Gregory Jones and Lynn Jones, my pastor and first lady. Thank you for your encouraging words and your biblical teaching during our Bible study and Sunday morning services and whenever I needed spiritual advice. I love you guys.

Kim Young. Kim, you and I became very close and very good friends. My friend, you have gone home to be with the Lord. I miss you so much. Every Sunday, I look at the church pew where you always sat. I love you, my friend.

Carl Young, my assistant pastor, the husband of my friend Kim Young, thank you for being the man of God that you are. God bless you.

Michael Pistore. Hey, buddy! I know you are up there in heaven looking down at me, smiling and saying, "Didn't I tell you, Irene, that your dream of becoming a successful fiction writer could come true?" Yes, it did, Mike. I just wish you were here to help me celebrate. I miss you and love you.

A new and dear friend to me, Fatema Marcus. Sis, you are one of the most caring people that I have ever met other than my best friend, Gladys. You are very special. I love talking with you, you always have something encouraging to say. I thank you and I love you. God bless you.

My crazy sister-in-law Rosie Lee! Girl, all I can say is that with you in my life, it has been a blast. I love you.

Last but not the least: George E. Davis Sr. Thank you for our lifelong friendship and the great conversations we have. Love you.

INTRODUCTION

I learned to seek faith in God at a very early age, from my mom's teaching of God's Word in the Holy Bible and mainly because of devastating, frightening situations that happened in my life. I believed that if I didn't have faith in God, the situations would have turned out very differently, and I probably would have lived the remainder of my life in a mental institution or an early death.

In the Bible, Hebrew 11:1 says, "Now faith is the substance of things hoped for, and the evidence of things not seen." I hoped that God would save my child's life and mine. I knew He would do just that because if He didn't, I would have lost my mind. Because of my faith in Him, God's Holy Spirit within me wouldn't let me believe anything else.

CHAPTER 1

A Lovely Day Started Out with Joy and Ended with Pain

It was a beautiful day. The sun was shining; the temperature was just right; everything was right within the world.

My phone rang. I answered; it was my loving husband wanting to know how our kids and I were doing. "Nothing exciting, honey."

He replied, "What's up? How about you and the children come to the base and we have lunch together!"

"Oh, honey, that sounds wonderful. What time do you want us to come?" I said.

"Now would be a great time to come to my office," he said.

With a smile, I replied, "Okay, honey."

Hearing the excitement in my voice, he said, "Be safe, baby."

With a chuckle, I said, "I will. Bye-bye."

My husband is in the United States Air Force and is currently stationed in the United States. I called out for our kids to come to the kitchen, saying that I have a surprise for them. They were in their playroom playing with their toys. I love hearing their little feet running around the house when their dad or I ask them to come here.

They came running eagerly to the kitchen to see what the surprise was. Looking up at me with their cute little faces, our son said, "Here we are, Mommy. What's the surprise?"

Our daughter said, "Yeah, Mommy, what's the surprise?"

I love my little ones so much, and their dad, my husband, does too. I squatted down to my little ones, kissed their little foreheads, sat them both on one of my knees, and replied, "How would you guys like to have lunch with Daddy today?"

They yelled, "Yeah!"

"Well, I guess that's a yes," I said as I laughed.

Our son said, "Well, come on, Mommy! Let's go have lunch with Daddy."

Our daughter said, "Yes, let's not keep Daddy waiting."

I smiled at them and said, "All right, you both can grab one toy to bring with you to see Daddy, okay? Just one."

"Okay, Mommy!" They ran to their playroom to get their one toy.

I love my family so much, and I thank God every day and night for them and for Him (God) to continue to bless and keep us well and healthy. I got our children in their seats and fastened their seat belts.

On our way to the base, the children were singing their little songs. I said to myself, "It is usual for this beautiful weather this time of the year and usually this time of morning right before lunch."

The traffic going to the base is usually pretty heavy but not today. As I was approaching the base gate, the young airman stepped out of his booth and waved me through.

When I parked in one of the parking spaces in front of my husband's office, I said, "Hey, guys, we are here at Daddy's job."

"Yay!" the children yelled.

I looked up, and here comes walking up my handsome husband looking so nice in his air force uniform. My husband looked at our children and me through the window with a huge smile on his face. He walked over to the right side of the car to the rear door where our children were and opened the door, saying, "Well, hello, family," giving our son a high five and kissed our daughter's little lips.

"Hi, Daddy!" our kids replied.

"Hi, guys. Did Mommy drive too fast?" my husband replied.

Laughing, our son said, "Yes, she did!"

Our daughter quickly replied, "No, she did not!"

My husband and I laughed. He said to our children, "Hey, guys, Daddy is going to close the car door and give some attention to that beautiful lady sitting in the front seat."

Our children laughed, and they knew their dad was talking about me. Our children went back to playing with their toy they brought with them.

My handsome husband came around to the driver's side of our car, where I was sitting, and opened the car door and said, "How are you, gorgeous lady?"

I said, "I'm good, my handsome man. How are you?"

He reached his hand out to me. I gave him my hand as he helped me get out of the car. He put his arms around my waist and said, "Holding you and looking at our beautiful children, I am good."

"Hey, guys, are you ready to eat?" he said to the kids.

"Yes!" they happily replied.

My husband turned to me and said, "Well, I guess that means they are ready to eat."

I said, "I think so, honey."

My husband walked me to the passenger side of our car as he opened the car door for me. I got inside of the car, and he fastened my seat belt and kissed my lips as we heard our kids giggling, and he said, "I love you, girl."

"I love you too," I replied.

He got inside the driver seat and drove off to the restaurant for our lunch.

When we walked into the restaurant, everyone's eyes were on us. I felt so blessed and happy to be having lunch with my family. I love my husband so much.

We all had burgers, fries, and a soda. The food was good, much better than I thought it would be.

This is the first time my husband has brought our children and me to this restaurant. He had talked about it to me before. Our children were enjoying their food and their toys.

My husband was holding my right hand. He kissed it and said, "I love you."

I said, "I love you too, honey. What time do you have to be back at work?"

"I have another hour. I told the captain that I was having a long overdue lunch with my family," he replied.

"Oh, honey, you are so sweet," I said.

He replied, "Thanks, baby. I love you all dearly, and I haven't been spending enough time with you guys."

"That's true, but I understand this is your job."

"Yes, it is," he said, "but a man needs to spend time with his family."

"I agree with you. I miss you so much when you are away, and so do our children."

He looked at me with watery eyes and said, "I know, baby. Once I earn this other stripe, that will increase my pay a lot, and with the stripe, I will pretty much call my own working hours, and I get to decide if I want to fly out working in other countries."

I wiped the tear that was rolling down his face and said, "I am so proud of you, honey, and you are the best husband."

"Well, baby, I try to be," he replied

After we finished eating our lunch, we sat outside, watching our children play. My husband and I talked about our children's future and what they would be when they grow up. It was so nice spending this time on a beautiful day with my husband and children.

My husband took my left hand, kissed it, and said, "I love you so much."

I said, "I love you too."

We looked into each other's eyes and smiled then started watching our children play.

CHAPTER 2

How Quickly Your Life Can Be Turned Upside Down

What is going on? I could not think clearly; my head was hurting; something wet was rolling down my face. I could hear voices, lots of voices; someone was holding on to me very tightly. I suddenly realized why my head was hurting so badly; I was screaming and saying, "No, no, no."

I see all of these people around me, and there was a hospital gurney with someone on it—a small person—and people in gray military hospital jackets standing near. It was my husband who was holding on to me so tightly and had our son in his left arm, holding him as he cried.

"Where is our daughter, and what is happening?" I asked my husband.

"There she is, sweetheart," he replied. "The doctors are working on her."

I felt my heart drop. "Working on her? What's wrong with her?"

Before my husband could answer me, I broke away from his arm and ran to my baby girl lying on that gurney, looking lifeless in my eyes. I said, "Oh, my God, please don't take my baby from me. I love her so much, God."

The doctors were still working on our daughter, putting in IVs, oxygen tubes in her little nose, and a blood pressure cuff. I was trying to put my arms around my baby girl, asking the doctors what was wrong, but the doctors said I would have to move back, and they would take good care of my baby. I was crying and praying to God to please save my baby girl's life for me.

My husband came over to me with our son in his left arm; our son had stopped crying. My husband took my right hand and gently pulled me into his right arm, saying, "Baby, the doctors will take good care of our child for us, okay? Come on and let the doctors do their jobs."

I laid my head on my husband's chest, crying my heart out for the life of our baby girl. One of the doctors said, "We have to get her to the hospital." The doctors began to wheel the gurney my baby girl was lying on.

I left my husband and our son standing there as I ran alongside the gurney with the doctors. Once the doctors had gotten my baby into the ambulance, I jumped into the hospital ambulance with the doctors.

My husband yelled, "I will meet you at the hospital, baby."

*****

I have never been so scared in my life, I thought to myself as I followed behind the ambulance. To see my daughter on the ground looking lifeless and to see how my wife reacted to the illness of our child tore at my heart. I'm just so happy I was here for my family.

Our son was in the back seat of our car and very quiet. When I reached the hospital emergency entry parking lot, I grabbed our son and rushed inside the hospital.

A hospital nurse took our son and me to the emergency waiting room. It took three hospital emergency nurses to bring my poor, worried wife to the waiting room, where our son and I were. She looked at me, saying, "Honey, they want to let me go with our baby daughter."

I held my wife in my arms, and I told the hospital nurses I would take care of my wife.

One of the nurses asked if the doctor should give my wife something to calm her nerves. "No, I just need to know if our child is all right."

One of the other nurses asked if they could get anything for our son. Our son said he wanted some juice, and the nurse said she would be right back.

I sat down with my wife, holding her in my arms, telling her that our daughter will be all right. "The doctor will be out soon to let us know what is wrong with our child. Just keep praying."

*****

I was so scared for our daughter. I did my best to take good care of my children and my husband. It seems like the doctors have been back there in the emergency room with our baby girl for hours. "Mommy, is sissy okay?"

I looked at my husband. He picked our son up and sat him on his lap and said, "Yes, little man, your sister will be fine. The doctors are taking good care of her. We will know something soon."

I was sitting there in the military hospital ER waiting room with my husband and our son, praying for God to really listen to me, to hear me asking Him to please save our daughter's life.

I am not in a strong relationship with God, but I will be after today because I need Him to heal our daughter, and I promised God that if He saved my daughter's life, I would go to church every Sunday (I don't know why I said that when I know that there would be times I would not be able to go to church every Sunday).

But I know God knows my heart, and He knows if I would or would not keep my word about going to church every Sunday if He healed my child, but at this moment, I do mean it, and I do hope I would keep my word to God about going to church every Sunday.

My family and I do go to church sometimes, and I do read the Bible sometimes, and with our daughter here in this hospital fighting for her life, my mind goes to a scripture in the Bible. I didn't know the book or the scriptures, but I do remember what was said, so I did some research and found them: "If you ask anything in my name I will do it" (John 14:14 KJV). I trust God to keep His promise to me, so this is why I asked Him in the name of Jesus to heal our daughter.

I am to walk by my faith in God and not by the sight of things I see happening: "We walk by faith not by sight" (2 Corinthians 5:7); in other words, my faith in God is so strong that I believe in Him and not what I am seeing and hearing that is going on with our daughter.

I heard footsteps coming down the hospital hallway. I opened my eyes, and it was the ER doctor walking toward us—my husband

and our son. My husband and I stood up. He had our son on his right hip and his left arm around my waist.

The doctor had a smile on his face, and that made my heart feel a little bit better. The doctor said, "Hey, guys, first of all, your daughter is good."

I said, "Oh thank God!"

My husband kissed my lips, and we laughed. I kissed our son's right cheek.

"Your daughter is resting very well. We had to do a battery test on her to find out what had happened. We knew from the beginning when we saw her and heard her breathing pattern that there was an issue with her lungs. I have given her medication to open up her lungs, and we still have her on oxygen and also IV to make sure she is getting the correct amount of nutrients in her body. The test result shows that your daughter had an asthma attack."

My husband and I looked at each other, and my husband asked the doctor, "Did you say asthma! Are you sure?"

"Well, I am pretty sure that is what happened, but we will do more tests. What was your daughter doing when the attack came on?"

My husband said, "She was playing in the grass at the restaurant. Did the grass she was playing in cause her to have the reaction?"

"Yes, it played a huge part in it. I will keep her overnight to make sure she can make it through the night without any episodes. I will make arrangements for you guys to stay the night here in the hospital with her. You can see her now. Come with me."

My husband has our son on his right hip, and he had his left arm around my waist, and we followed the doctor to where our daughter was.

I was so excited. I wanted to see our daughter so badly so I could let her know that Mommy, Dad, and her little brother love her. We are here, and she will get well.

The smell of the hospital's cleaning solutions, the medications, and food mixed together, I was getting sick to my stomach. And the sounds of the different medical machines in the ICU unit and some of the patients crying and moaning made me more scared inside of my heart and stomach and worried for them.

I wanted to tell them to read John 16:24. It reads, "Until now you have asked nothing in My Name. Ask, and you will receive, that your joy may be full." Ask God for what you want Him to do for you in the name of His Son Jesus Christ. I did.

Hebrew 11:1 reads, "Now faith is the substance of things hoped for and the evidence of things not seen." My faith is my hope (which is in God) that lets me know in my heart that even though I can't see what God is doing to heal our daughter, I know that He will (the unseen).

When the doctor pulled the curtain back, all those medical machines were humming. Doctors and nurses were attending different patients, adjusting their oxygen masks, taking their blood pressure, and drawing blood. To the right of the room in a bed with light-green sheets over a tiny body with a tiny oxygen mask on her little face was our daughter with an IV in her little left arm. Her eyes were closed, and I could barely see her breathing.

I was so scared and feeling so bad because I couldn't take the pain and suffering of our daughter. I felt as if I had failed her, my husband, and our son as a good mother. I could not keep myself from crying.

The doctor said, "Your daughter is fine, and she is resting. I want her to rest. Her little body is tired, and she needs the rest. I will be back to let you know when your daughter's room is ready.

I said, "Thank you, doctor."

He said, "You're welcome," and left the hospital ER space where our daughter was.

I took a deep breath, walked over to our daughter's hospital bed, and kissed her little cheek and said, "Baby, Mom is here, so is Dad and brother, and we love you, and you will be well soon, okay?"

Her dad with her brother still in his arm on his right hip bent over and kissed our daughter's cheek and said, "Baby girl, Dad is here. You are going to be all right. We love you so much."

Our son bent over to his little sister and said, "Hey, sissy, this is your brother. Are you all right?" Our son didn't understand why his sissy wasn't answering him.

I told our son, "Yes, baby, she is asleep right now. The doctor said she needs to rest. She will be able to talk to you tomorrow, okay?"

"Okay, Mom," he replied.

I kissed our son's right cheek, and he laid his little head on his dad's right shoulder. I could see our son's little eyes slowly closing. It has been a very scary, confusing, and tiring day for him.

It was about fifteen minutes later when our daughter's doctor came and told us that our daughter's hospital room was ready for us and that everything was set up for us too. Our son slowly opened his sleepy eyes with his head on his dad's right shoulder. The doctor looked at our son and said, "Little man, I will have the nurse bring you a pair of Mickey Mouse pj's. Would you like that?"

Our son had a huge smile on his face, and with enthusiasm, he said, "Yes, doctor, I would like that."

We all laughed when the doctor gave our son a high five.

The nurse's assistant came to our daughter's room and said that he was here to take our daughter to her room and asked us to follow him. He wheeled our daughter's ICU hospital bed onto the elevator, saying that we could come with him. Our daughter's doctor said he would meet us in our daughter's room later.

I was so happy our daughter was able to go to her own hospital room. Our daughter's room was in the pediatrics unit, where the care of infants and children are taken care of.

When we got to our daughter's hospital room, the nurse assisted her nurse's assistant with placing our daughter on to her new hospital bed. The room was very large. The staff had set up a small bed for our son and a full-size bed for my husband and me. There was a full-size bathroom with a large bathtub shower and all the personal things we needed for our bathing tonight and tomorrow morning. Across the foot of the bed my husband and I were to sleep in were two pairs of pj's, a pair for me and a pair for my husband.

I thanked the nurse and her nurse's assistant for everything. My husband held our son over to his little sister so he could give her a kiss. Our poor little daughter was sleeping peacefully. I sat in one of the chairs at our daughter's bedside and held her right hand, praying, thanking God for bringing life back to our daughter.

There was a knock on our daughter's hospital room door. I got up to open the door, and my husband and our son were in the bathroom. I opened the door, and it was the nutritionist with a list for me to fill out for what we wanted for dinner tonight and breakfast tomorrow morning. "Hi, how are you?"

I said, "I'm good, how are you?"

She said, "I am good. This is the list for you to fill out for your meals for this evening and tomorrow morning's breakfast."

I filled out the menu and thanked her. She said, "You're welcome. Your food will be here as soon as it is ready, okay? Thanks."

I could hear the water running from the shower in the bathroom where my son and husband were taking their shower. There was a knock on our daughter's hospital room door. It was my daughter's doctor and his nurse. The doctor checked my daughter's vital signs and said they were good, then he asked the nurse to get a blood sample from our daughter.

When the nurse rubbed my daughter's tiny arm with the alcohol pad to clean the area so she could insert the needle so she could draw the blood, my daughter moved her arm a bit and took a deep breath but didn't wake up.

The nurse was very gentle with my daughter. She said, "I'm sorry, baby girl. I am finished and hopefully I won't have to take any blood from you again."

I asked my daughter's doctor why my daughter is still sleeping. He said he had given her some medication so she could sleep and rest and that her body needs the rest.

My husband and son came from the bathroom with their pj's and bedroom slippers on. My husband and our son were looking at the doctor and nurse with fear in their eyes, walking over to where I was standing near our daughter's hospital bed. My husband asked the doctor how our daughter was doing, and the doctor said, "She is doing very well. She might be able to go home later tomorrow, and if she is sure, make her a follow up appointment with her primary doctor. She is resting well, and you guys need to get a good night's sleep after your dinner."

We thanked the doctor and said good night to him and his nurse.

The nurse said if we needed anything, please let her know and said good night and left our daughter's hospital room with the doctor.

I kissed our daughter, our son, and my husband, and I went to the bathroom to get my shower and get ready for dinner.

I was very tired. The hot water flowing from the showerhead felt so wonderful on my tired body I closed my eyes, letting the warm water hit my face. I cried and prayed, thanking God for His blessing, taking care of our daughter for us. I was so scared and sick in my stomach from the pain when I thought I had lost my baby.

When I came from the bathroom, my husband and our son were sitting at the dining room table, waiting for me so we could have our dinner. I said, "Oh my goodness, I hope I didn't keep you guys waiting too long."

My husband said, "No, you didn't, baby. The food just got here a few seconds ago."

"Oh, great." I sat down at the dining room table with my husband and our son.

My husband blessed our food, and we ate.

After we finished our dinner, I rang the nurses' station to let her know that we had finished our dinner, and someone could come and get the dishes. The nurse came to our daughter's hospital room and got the cart that our finished dishes were on after she did a check on our daughter.

My husband took our son to the bathroom so he could pee before he went to bed. After my husband and son had finished in the bathroom, I went in the bathroom, brushed my teeth, and rinsed my mouth.

When I went back into our daughter's room, my little family were all sleeping so peacefully. I kissed my daughter and son again, and in my quite voice, I said, "Good night, and I love you," to them.

I eased into bed with my husband, and I got comfortable next to him. He kissed the back of my neck and asked me if I was okay.

"Oh, honey, I didn't mean to wake you."

He said, "Baby, you didn't wake me. I was praying, thanking God for the good health of our son and for getting our daughter well and for a wonderful loving wife."

"Oh, thank you, honey. I thank God for you, my loving husband, and our children."

We said good night and said that we loved each other.

CHAPTER 3

A Precious Surprise

I don't know how soon my husband and I fell asleep last night. I guess I slept well last night. This morning, the smell of fresh coffee and the snoring of our son and my husband woke me up. I bet I got up at least ten times last night, checking on our sick daughter. I eased from the bed, trying not to wake my husband. I checked on our daughter, and she was still sleeping. I kissed her forehead and told her I love her.

I went over to our son; he was sleeping. I kissed his forehead and told him that I love him. Then I went to the bathroom, showered, brushed my teeth, rinsed my mouth, and got dressed.

When I came back into our daughter's hospital room, I was so happy and surprised at what I saw! Our daughter was sitting up in her hospital bed, looking at her sleeping dad and her sleeping brother. I was so excited. I said in my loud voice, "Good morning, my sweet baby girl!"

She looked at me, smiling, and said, "Good morning, Mommy."

I ran over to her hospital bed, kissed her right cheek, held her in my arms gently so I wouldn't pull her IV out. "How are you feeling, sweetheart?"

"I feel good, Mommy."

I guess my excitement and our daughter's talking woke my husband and our son up. My husband said, "Well, well, little princess, it's about time you woke up."

And our son rushed over to our daughter's bedside. Her little brother said, "Hi, sissy, are you okay?"

She smiled at him and said, "I am good. Are you okay?"

He said, "Yes. If you are okay, I am okay."

My husband picked our son up so he could give his little sister a hug. They hugged each other, then my husband sat our son on the bed beside our daughter and kissed our daughter's right cheek, hugged her gently, and told her he loved her.

Our son looked at his dad like, "What about me?"

Then my husband said, "I love you too."

He looked at me and said, "Good morning, baby. I love you three."

We all laughed.

I said, "I love you," then he asked me how I was doing. "I am good now that this little sweet thing—our daughter—is doing better. How are you this morning?"

He said, "I am better too now that our daughter is doing much better."

There was a knock on our daughter's door. I said, "Come in." It was the nurse coming to check on our daughter. She had a cart with coffee, creamer, and sugar for me and my husband and orange juices for the children.

The nurse said, "Good morning, everyone. And look at you, little one." She was referring to our daughter. "Here is some coffee for you two [me and my husband] and juices for the little ones."

We said, "Thank you, nurse.

"Oh, you're welcome." The nurse looked at our daughter and said, "You are looking well this morning. How do you feel?"

Our daughter said, "I feel good."

The nurse said, "Is it okay if I check you over and see how well you are doing? I noticed you slept well last night."

"Yes, I did."

The nurse removed the oxygen tube from our daughter's nose then turned the oxygen off, checked her blood pressure and temperature, listened to her heart, and checked her breathing. The nurse had our daughter blow into this tube thing that had a little ball inside of it. She said she wanted to check our daughter's lung capacity.

Our daughter blew so hard, the little ball went all the way to the top of the plastic container, and we all laughed. The nurse said, "My goodness, our [talking about our daughter] little lungs are perfect. That is good. Can you blow into the tube two more times for me?"

"Yes." Our daughter blew into the tube two more times, but each time, the little ball wouldn't go even halfway up the container.

The nurse said, "It's okay, sweetie. Would you care for some juice?"

"Yes."

The nurse gave our daughter a glass of orange juice and said, "I hope this will hold you guys up until breakfast gets here. I will let your doctor know how you are doing, sweetheart." The nurse put the oxygen tube back in our daughter's nose and turned the oxygen back on.

We thanked the nurse for everything she said. We were welcome, and if we needed anything, let her know, and she left our daughter's hospital room.

My husband said to our son, "Well, little sport, are you ready for your shower?"

Eagerly, he said, "Yes, Daddy."

My husband and our son went to the bathroom for their shower.

Our daughter had finished her orange juice and was lying back on her hospital bed pillow. I was sipping my delicious coffee, and in my mind, I was giving thanks to God for taking care of our child for us.

My husband and our son came from the bathroom all showered and dressed. I asked our son, "Sport, did you brush your teeth good for Daddy?"

"Yes, Mommy, I did."

There was a knock on our daughter's hospital room door. My husband went over to the door and opened it, and it was the kitchen staff with our breakfast. She said, "Good morning!"

We all said, "Good morning."

"I have your breakfast for you." She took our daughter's food tray off first and sat it on her bed table, set her food up for her, then helped our daughter sit up in bed comfortably so she could eat her breakfast. Then she sat our son's food tray on the dining table, then my food tray, and then my husband's.

We thanked her, and she said, "You are welcome. Is there anything else I could get for any of you?"

My husband looked at me. I looked at him, and we said, "No, thank you. Everything is fine."

She said, "Okay, enjoy your breakfast," and she left the room.

My husband blessed our food. The food was delicious. I had scrambled eggs, two slices of wheat toast with grape jelly, two pieces of bacon, a glass of orange juice, and another cup of coffee. My husband had three scrambled eggs, one slice of ham, four pieces of bacon, grits, two slices of wheat toast with grape jelly, a glass of orange juice, and another cup of coffee. Our son had a small bowl of Cap'n Crunch cereal, a glass of milk, a small glass of orange juice, one piece of bacon, and one slice of wheat toast. Our daughter had a small bowl of oatmeal, one slice of wheat toast, and a glass of milk.

After breakfast, our daughter went to sleep, and our son watched TV. My husband and I talked about our daughter's going home from the hospital and about making her a follow-up appointment with her pediatrician and hoped my husband would be able to be home with us through all of this.

There was a light knock on my daughter's hospital room door. It was our daughter's doctor, who asked if he could come in. I said, "Yes, doctor, you may come in."

He was smiling and said, "Good morning. How are we feeling this morning?" looking and talking to our daughter.

Our daughter smiled at her doctor and said, "I feel good."

He said, "I am happy you feel great."

My husband sat straight up on the sofa, listening to the doctor. Our daughter's doctor said that it is medically confirmed that our daughter has a serious case of asthma. My husband said, "She really does have *asthma!* How could she have asthma? I know you said that the grass she played in yesterday was partly to blame for the asthma attack. Can you fix it? What is this asthma?"

The doctor said, "Well, asthma is a chronic disorder characterized by wheezing, coughing, difficulty in breathing, and a suffocating feeling. I had a consultation with an allergy specialist, and she told me what medication to give to your daughter. I have, and it appears that the medication is working for her, but as for fixing her asthma condition, I will let the allergy specialist work with you with that, okay? I made an appointment with the allergy specialist for your daughter. I hope that's okay with you guys."

I said, "Yes, it's fine, doctor."

He said, "The doctor would do a series of allergy tests on our daughter to see exactly what she is allergic to."

My husband asked the doctor if our daughter would outgrow asthma. The doctor said, "It is a great chance that she would, given she is very young and pretty much healthy other than the asthma and if we make sure we follow her asthma specialist's instructions. I would like to keep her here in the hospital one more night to see how well she will do without the oxygen. I am going to take her off the oxygen since her breathing sounds good."

I said, "That's fine, doctor. We want to make sure our daughter is well before we take her from the hospital."

He said, "Great."

There was a knock on our daughter's hospital room door. The doctor opened the door, and it was the food person with our breakfast. The doctor said, "Please come in. I'm sure everyone here is hungry."

Our son said, "Yes, I am."

We all laughed.

The food server gave our daughter her food first, then our son, then me and my husband and said for us to enjoy. I said, "We will, and thank you."

He said we were welcome and left the room.

I was so happy that our daughter had an appetite. I opened her orange juice for her buttered toast and put a little sugar and butter in her oatmeal. My husband helped our son with his breakfast. He had orange toast milk and cold cereal. I had bacon, scrambled eggs, toast and grape jelly, coffee, and orange juice. My husband had bacon, ham, eggs, grits, toast and jelly, coffee, and orange juice. The food was delicious. It was so funny to me that nobody was saying a word, just enjoying their breakfast.

Just as we were finishing our meal, there was a knock on the door. My husband got up and opened the door. It was our daughter's nurse. She said, "Oh, good morning. My timing is bad. I'm sorry to interrupt your breakfast."

I said, "No problem. We are finishing up."

She said, "Are you sure?"

I said, "Yes, I'm sure."

The nurse looked at our daughter and asked, "How are you this morning, sweetheart?"

Our daughter said, "I feel good."

The nurse told our daughter that she would not be poking her little arm this morning, and our daughter said, "Oh, thank you."

The nurse said, "You are welcome, sweetheart, but I am going to check your vital signs, okay?"

Our daughter said, "Okay."

After the nurse finished with our daughter, she said everything is looking good and that our daughter's doctor has everything arranged for us to spend another night here at the hospital with our daughter. She looked at our son and said, "Hi, little man, could I get you anything?"

Our son said, "Hi, yes. I want a toy."

We all laughed, and the nurse said, "Okay, sir, I will get you a toy.

Our son said, "Thank you, Ms. Nurse."

We all laughed again, and the nurse said, "You are welcome, darling," and left the room.

I gave my husband a list of items to get from our home to bring to the hospital. My husband looked at my list then looked at me and said, "Baby, all of this, the hospital staff will think we are moving in."

I laughed and said, "Honey, they will not."

He looked at me. He had a little frown on his handsome face and said, "Okay, baby," then he asked our son if he wanted to go with him, and he said, "Yes, Daddy."

My husband helped our son with his bath and dressed him when he had showered and dressed. My husband picked up our son and put him in bed beside our daughter, our son's little sick sister, and he played with them. I stood in the background, tears coming from my eyes dropping on my cheeks; the tears were from thankfulness, happiness, and how much I loved and thanked God for the life of our daughter and my loving family. I didn't want my family to see me crying, so I went to the bathroom, showered, brushed my teeth, and rinsed my mouth.

When I went into the bedroom, our baby daughter had fallen asleep, and my husband and son were watching TV with the volume low so it wouldn't disturb our daughter's sleep.

I was dressed. I said in my low voice to my husband and our son, "So you guys tired her out."

Our son said, "No, Mom, she just went to sleep."

I said, "Oh, okay, sweetie. Thank you."

My husband said, "Yes, we did. I love her so much, and I'm so happy that she is getting well."

"I am too, honey." I gave my husband and our son a kiss and told my husband to be safe.

"I will, baby." He kissed my lips, picked up our son, and said, "Okay, baby, we will see you girls soon."

"Okay, honey, I will see you when you guys get back," and they left.

I kissed our daughter's little right cheek, sat down on the little sofa, and prayed to God, thanking Him for His love and blessing.

There was a light knock on our daughter's hospital room door. I got up quietly and opened the door. It was our daughter's nurse's assistant coming to give our daughter her bath.

The nurse's assistant was very gentle with our daughter, and our daughter must have really enjoyed her warm bath because she did not wake up during the entire bath.

The nurse's assistant put a clean nightgown on her and a pair of clean socks on her little feet and changed her bedding with clean bedding and asked me if there were anything else I needed her to do for my daughter or me. I said, "Thank you, no. We are good, and thank you for being so caring and gentle with my baby girl. I could tell she really enjoyed the bath you gave her. Thank you again."

"You're welcome."

The nurse's assistant cleaned up everything around my daughter's bed, brought clean drinking glasses and fresh water, and left the room.

I kissed my daughter's forehead and told her that I love her. She said, "I love you too, Mommy." She closed her eyes and went to sleep.

I went back to the little sofa, got a blanket, lay down, put the blanket over me, got comfortable, and there was a knock on the door.

I got up and opened the door, and it was housekeeping here to clean our daughter's room and said she had brought fresh bedding and towels for us and asked, "Is it okay if I cleaned?"

"Yes. Thank you."

"I will be quiet so I won't wake your daughter."

"Thank you."

I lay back down on the sofa, put the blanket over me, and waited for the cleaning lady to finish before I fell asleep.

The cleaning products the cleaning lady was using had a nice, clean smell. She was very nice. She asked if there was anything else I needed for my daughter. "No, there isn't. Thanks and have a good day."

She said, "You're welcome. If you need anything, just ring for your nurse. Bye." She left the room.

My daughter was sleeping so peacefully, and I was feeling so blessed and at peace. "These things I have spoken to you that in Me you may have peace. In the world you will have tribulation; but be of good cheer, I have overcome the world" (John 16:33 KJV). I thank

God for His Son Jesus Christ, who gave His life for us so that we might have a second chance at life on this earth.

I was getting very sleepy, and I could hardly keep my eyes open. I looked over at my daughter in her hospital bed to make sure she was resting well, and where I pulled the blanket over me and up to my neck, it was warm and felt good to my body. I fell asleep.

CHAPTER 4

A Huge Scare

When I woke up from my nap, I was surprised that the room was so quiet. My husband and our son weren't back. I sat up on the sofa and looked toward my daughter's bed, and it was empty. I panicked, jumped from the sofa, ran to my baby's bed, and she was gone. I ran out the room into the hallway, yelling to the nurses, "Where is my daughter?"

At first, the nurses' facial expressions were of fear, then the four nurses came to me, putting their arms around me, saying, "It's okay, honey. Your baby is fine. She is in the playroom, playing with the other children."

I said, "Oh my god, thank you. I didn't know what had happened to her."

One of the nurses said, "We are so sorry. You were sleeping so peacefully. We didn't want to wake you. You haven't been sleeping ever since your daughter has been here in this hospital."

One of the nurses said she would take me to my daughter. When the nurse and I got to the playroom, my daughter saw me, smiling. She ran to me and put her little arms around my waist, saying, "Hi, Mom, did you sleep well?"

I smiled and said, "Yes, I did, baby. Are you having fun?"

"Yes, Mom." She let go of my waist and ran back to play with the children.

I looked at my wristwatch, and it was past lunch, and my husband and our son are not back from our home with the personal item I asked him to get. I asked my daughter's nurse if she is okay playing, and she said, "Yes, she is fine. See the nurses in here? The children are fine. Are you okay?"

I looked at the nurse and took a deep breath and said, "Yes, I am, and thank you."

"You're welcome. I will get back to my station, okay? See you later."

"Okay, nurse."

I looked around in the children's playroom, and I saw other parents looking at their children. I was praying that everything was good with my husband and our son. I am sure if something were wrong, my husband would have called me.

My daughter came to me rubbing her eyes. "Are you sleepy, honey?"

"Yes, Mom, I am tired."

"Okay, sweetie, we will go to your room and put you to bed so you can get a nap."

One of the nurses in the playroom was watching me and my daughter. Then the nurse came over to us with a wheelchair and asked if my daughter was tired, and she said yes. "Okay, I will take you and Mom to your room." She picked my daughter up and sat her in the wheelchair, and away we went to my daughter's room.

When we got to my daughter's hospital room, I was surprised and happy to see my son and my husband. They rushed over to us, and my husband asked if everything was okay.

Our daughter said, "Yes, Daddy. We were in the playroom."

Our son's eyes got huge, and he said, "I want to go to the playroom."

I said, "Maybe tomorrow, sweetie. Did you get your nap when you and Daddy were home?"

My husband said, "Yes, he did. That's why it took us so long to get back to the hospital." Then my husband picked up our daughter from the wheelchair and put her on her hospital bed and pulled the covers up over her.

The nurse took the wheelchair. I said, "Thank you, nurse."

"You're, welcome. Do you need anything else?"

"No, thank you."

She left the room.

My husband kissed our daughter on her forehead and said, "Daddy loves you, baby girl," then he looked at me and said, "I love you too, baby."

I said, "I love you too, honey."

Our son was watching TV, and our daughter's eyes were closed. She had fallen asleep. I walked over to my husband and put my arms around his shoulders. He put his arms around my waist. He whispered in my right ear, "I gave our neighbors and my job an update on our daughter's condition."

Then there was a knock on the door. My husband let go of my waist and answered the door. It was our dinner. I filled out the menu last night. I ordered my husband what he wanted, which was two deep-fried pork chops, mashed potatoes with sour cream, butter and brown gravy, butter bread, green beans, a slice of banana cream pie, and a strawberry soda. The children and I had the same thing, except we had one pork chop, and the children had apple juice, and I had a hot cup of tea.

The food was delicious, and I was hungry. I had missed lunch, and it was too close to dinner for me to eat anything, and I needed and enjoyed the nap I had had.

After we had finished our dinner, my husband put our son in bed with our daughter so they could play before bedtime; he told them that they had thirty minutes to play. My husband and I sat on the little sofa, talking about our daughter's doctor appointment with the asthma specialist. My husband said to me, "Baby, I will be here at home for our daughter's doctor appointment."

"Oh, honey, you will? I am so happy. Thank you, honey."

"Come on, baby. You don't have to thank me for being here for my family."

"I know, honey, but I didn't know if you would have to fly out or not. It's around this time of the year you usually fly out."

"That's true, but our sick daughter needs us to be together at this time."

"Yes, she does, honey, and I need you too."

There was a knock on the door. My husband got up and opened the door. It was our daughter's doctor. "Good evening, guys." Looking at our daughter, the doctor said, "How is my little patient this evening?"

"I am fine. I am playing with my doll my daddy bought me."

Her doctor said, "Could you ask your doll if I could check you out?"

She laughed. "You don't have to ask her to ask me."

We all laughed.

"Okay, may I check your heart and your lungs?"

Our daughter said, "Yes."

So the doctor listened to our daughter's heart and listened to see if her lungs were clear. "Hey, young lady, everything sounds good."

Our son was watching every move the doctor made toward his little sister. The doctor looked at our son and asked him if he could listen to his heart? Our son smiled and said yes with excitement. The doctor placed his stethoscope on our son's little chest and said, "Wow, you have a strong heartbeat. That is great."

Our son asked the doctor, "Could I listen to your heartbeat?"

The doctor laughed and said, "Sure you can."

Our son put the little things in his ears, placed the stethoscope on the doctor's chest, and his eyes widened with excitement and said, "Wow, doctor, you have a very strong heartbeat."

We all laughed.

The doctor said, "Thank you."

"You are a welcome, doctor."

The doctor said, "Well, if her vitals stay the same, she may be able to go home some time tomorrow."

"Oh, thank you, doctor. That would be great."

"You're welcome. Is there anything you guys need?"

"No, I can't think of anything. Honey?"

"No. Thanks, doc."

And the doctor left.

My husband told our children that they only had five minutes left to play before they would have to bathe and go to bed.

There was a knock on the door. My husband looked at me, went to the door, opened it, and said, "Please come in."

It was the evening staff. "Hi, I am here to see if you need your beds turned down."

My husband looked at me, and I said, "Oh, no, but thank you for checking with us."

"You're welcome. Do you need anything for your bathroom?"

"No. It was taken care of this morning."

"Okay, good night."

We said, "good night."

My husband said, "Wow, it seems like we are at a five-star hotel."

"Yes, it does. Thank God for such great treatment from the doctors and staff here at this wonderful hospital. I thanked God for the great doctors here and nurses for taking great care of our daughter."

"I do too, baby."

My husband said, "Okay, little man, it is time for your shower so you can get to bed. You have had a long day today."

My husband showered our son, and I bathed our daughter.

After we all bathed and showered, we went over to our daughter's bed, held hands and said our prayers together, gave each other a kiss, and said good night. My husband pulled the covers up over our daughter, put our son in his bed.

My husband and I got in bed. I took a deep breath and said good night to my husband. He said, "Good night, baby. I love you."

I said, "I love you too."

CHAPTER 5

A Very Scary Disappointment

I wasn't sure if I was dreaming or if this was reality I was hearing. I hear what appears to be someone having difficulty breathing, moaning, and wheezing. I thought about our daughter and became clearly awake. I looked over at our daughter's hospital bed, and there she was, sitting up in her bed, trying to breathe. I jumped from my bed, ran over to her, and put my arms around her to let her know that I am here for her, and at the same time, I was pressing the button to the nurse's station.

I told our daughter to try and slow down her breathing, and our daughter's bedroom door immediately opened, and there were four nurses rushing into our daughter's room with medical machines. One nurse checked our daughter's eyes. Her eyes were closed now, and I could only see the white of her eyes. One of the nurses inserted a needle into our daughter's left arm, another nurse hung an IV bag on the IV pole, and another nurse put the oxygen mask over our daughter's little face.

I was crying, asking the nurses what was wrong with our daughter. My husband had his arms around my waist, saying she will be all right. "Baby, let the nurses do their job."

I was so happy when our daughter's breathing became normal, and she wasn't wheezing anymore. The nurse in charge looked at me and my husband and said that our daughter had had an asthma attack.

She called the lab department and asked if someone would come up to our daughter's room and draw some blood. "She just had an asthma attack, and we need to find out what she ate or drank that brought on the attack."

A few seconds later, our daughter's bedroom door opened, and it was her doctor. "Hey, what's going on here? I got a call that my little patient was in distress."

And the nurse in charge said, "Yes, doctor. She had an asthma attack. Something she drank or ate caused the reaction."

"Okay, I see you have everything taken care of with the proper IV, oxygen, and—"

"Yes, doctor, and I have called for the lab technician to come up and draw some blood and do some testing to see what caused her reaction."

"Great job, nurse."

"Thank you, doctor."

There was a knock on the door. A nurse opened the door. It was the lab technician there to draw blood from our daughter so she could do the testing. Our daughter's doctor used his stethoscope to listen to our daughter's heart and her chest to see if her lungs were clearing. "Well, her heartbeat is good and strong and normal, but her lungs are still a bit congested, but that will clear up after she has gotten enough of the medication into her system."

The doctor said, "Nurse, call me as soon as you get the results from the lab on her blood test, okay?"

"Yes, doctor."

"Call me even if I am at home."

"Will do, doctor."

Our daughter's doctor looked at me and my husband and said, "Okay, guys, things are under control, but we just need to find out what caused the reaction. She is resting right now. I want her to get as much sleep and rest as possible, okay? She will be out for a while, but if there's any changes, let the nurse know okay?"

I said, "Okay, doctor."

My husband said, "Thank you, doctor."

He said, "You're welcome. I will see you guys later. Take care."

"Okay, doctor."

Our daughter's doctor left her room.

The nurse in charge checked our daughter's oxygen meter gauge and said, "She is resting well. If you need anything, please let us know, okay?"

"Thank you, nurses, and we will. I hope we don't need to bother you."

"Oh, no, sweetie, there is no bother. This is what we are here for, to take care of our patients and their families."

I said, "Thanks."

The nurses left our daughter's hospital room. Thank God all the commotions with our daughter's asthma attack didn't wake our son from his sleep.

My husband took my right hand, and we walked over to our daughter's hospital bed. She was sleeping, and her breathing appears to be normal because of the oxygen and medications. We prayed to God again, thanking Him for taking care of our daughter again. I remembered the verses in the Holy Bible.

> Teaching them to observe all things whatsoever I have commanded you: and, lo, I am with you always, even unto the end of the world. Amen. (Matthew 28:20)

> And it came to pass, that, as he was praying in a certain place, when he ceased, one of his disciples said unto him, Lord, teach us to pray, as John also taught his disciples. And he said unto them, when ye pray, say, Our Father which art in heaven, Hallowed be thy name. (Luke 11:1–2 NRSV)

I thought about what Jesus had said in John 16:24: "Until now have ye asked nothing in my name: ask, and ye shall receive, that your joy may be full." I did that in my prayers to God "in the name of Jesus," but I had to learn how to do what Matthew 6:33 said to do: "But seek ye first the kingdom of God, and his righteousness; and all these things shall be added unto you." It is such a great comfort to read God's reassuring words, knowing that no matter what you may be going through, God is always there to help you through it.

My husband and I kissed our little girl's forehead and whispered in her right ear that we love her and that she will get well soon so she could go home. My husband and I went over to our son's bed. He was sleeping like an angel; we kissed his little right cheek and asked God to continue taking care of our son as well as our daughter.

My husband kissed my lips and said, "Baby, let's get some sleep."

We went to our bed and said our prayers again, and I asked God to keep our daughter alive and well and our son and my husband well and healthy. Keep me well and healthy so I could take care of our children and my husband. I said, "Honey, I hope our food comes late."

He said, "I do too."

We went to bed.

The next morning, I woke up a little before 8:30 a.m. I went over to our daughter's hospital bed; she was still sleeping, and her breathing appeared to be normal even though she was still on the oxygen. The tears came down my cheeks, not from sadness but from joy, joy that my child was still alive.

I know that every mother can relate to how I am feeling. Our child or children are our life; they mean everything to us, and it is very scary to a mother when she feels that the life or health of her child or children are at stake. God is a good God.

In the Bible, it says that we will have tribulations: "I have said these things to you, that in me you may have peace. In the world you will have tribulation. But take heart; I have overcome the world" (John 16:33).

I went to the bathroom, brushed my teeth, rinsed my mouth with our mint mouthwash, got a good hot shower, and got dressed. Just as I was coming from the bathroom, there was a light knock on our daughter's door. I went over to the door and opened it. It was our daughter's doctor; he said in a low tone, talking about our daughter, "Good morning. How is our little patient this morning?"

I said, "Good morning," in my low tone. "She is sleeping well. It appears her breathing is good."

The doctor said, "That's good. Let me check her vitals."

The doctor and I walked over to my daughter's bedside. He checked her IV in her arm; he checked her oxygen and listened to her heart and lungs. My daughter slept through the whole exam. The doctor turned toward me with a smile on his face and said, "Everything looks and sounds good. She is out of the woods, so to speak. We got her lab test results back last night."

My eyes open wide, and I said, "You did!" I could tell from the expression on the doctor's face that he felt that I thought he thought that I was a bad mother for sleeping through the night, not staying awake to hear what my daughter's test results would be.

The doctor immediately said, "Oh, don't feel bad because you didn't hear us come in here last night. We were quite like little mice because we didn't want to wake you guys. You are a wonderful mother, and don't let anyone tell you differently.

"Hey, you were exhausted. You needed the sleep and rest. Look when your daughter goes home, you will have to take care of her on your own unless you need us for something."

I said, "Oh, thank you, doctor. This is a relief. I didn't want you—"

He cut me off. "You don't have to say it. As I said, you are a wonderful mother." The doctor gave me a quick reassuring hug.

My husband woke up and said, "Good morning. How is our daughter doing when her lab results came back?"

Our daughter's doctor said, "Good morning, and yes, her results have come back, and I was just about to ask your wife if she wanted to wake you so you could hear the results together."

My husband said, "Yes, I would. Thank you, doctor." My husband got out of bed, put on his bathrobe and slippers, came over to our daughter's bed beside me, and took my left hand. "Okay, doctor, we are ready."

"Your daughter's test results reveal that she had an allergic reaction to something. That could be anything from peanuts, milk, dust, cigarette smoke, and certain fragrance. That could range from lotion, powder, perfume and definitely grass.

"When she sees her allergy specialist, she will run a battery of food and other tests on her, and that will give us a good sense of most, if not all, the things your daughter is allergic to."

My husband asked the doctor why she is still sleeping.

"She is still sleeping because I gave her some medication, the same medication I gave her when she was first admitted into the hospital to make her rest and sleep. Her little body needs it. Don't worry. She is fine. She will wake up shortly and in good spirits.

"I will be back in about two hours to check on her, and if things are still good as they are now, I will remove the heart monitor, the oxygen, the IV, and her urinary catheter."

I said, "Okay, doctor, thank you so much."

He said, "You're welcome, but I'm sorry you guys will have to stay another night here in this hospital with us. I want to keep her here for further observations, unless you'd rather go home tonight. Your daughter is in great hands."

My husband said, "Oh, no problem, doctor. We will stay here with our child."

I said, "I agree with my husband, doctor, that we will stay here in the hospital with our child."

"Good. I will let the staff know that you will be here with us for another night. Your breakfast should be here shortly. I will see you guys later."

My husband thanked the doctor.

The doctor looked over at our son, who was sitting up in his bed looking at us. The doctor said, "Good morning, little man."

And our son said, "Good morning. Good morning, Mom and Dad."

We said, "Good morning, son. How are you this morning?"

He said, "Good. How is sissy?"

"Sissy is good. She is still sleeping."

"Dad, why do sissy sleep so much?"

My husband said, "Your sister was very sick—problem with her breathing—so the good doctor here"—pointing at our daughter's doctor—"gave your sister some medication so she could rest and get lots of sleep so she can get well."

Our son was looking at his dad as if he was really understanding what his dad was telling him about his sister's illness. "Okay, Dad, then we have to be quiet so we don't wake her."

My husband said, "Are you all right, son?" then he walked over to our son's bed and picked him up. "I am so proud of you, son. You are really growing up."

Our son smiled and hugged his dad.

The doctor told our son to enjoy his breakfast when it came. He had the kitchen to fix something special! Our son's eyes got huge. "Thank you, doctor."

"You're welcome, little man," and the doctor left our daughter's hospital room.

My husband asked me how I was feeling this morning. "I'm fine. How are you?"

He said, "I'm good."

My husband said, "Okay, little man, it is time for us to get to the bathroom so we can get our shower and get dressed before our breakfast."

"Okay, Dad. I want to see my surprise the doctor has for me."

My husband and I laughed. My husband and son went to the bathroom.

I got my daughter's washbasin, filled it with warm water, washed her face and hands, and bathed her little body. I didn't use any soap or lotion on her body. I put a clean fresh nightgown on her and clean, fresh socks on her feet. She opened her little eyes with a beautiful smile on her face and said, "Hi, Mommy!"

"Hi, baby, how are you?"

"I'm good."

"Great!" I gave her a big hug and kiss on her right cheek and said, "I love you, sweetheart."

"I love you too, Mommy."

I got my daughter's toothbrush, toothpaste, and mouthwash from her bed drawer. I helped her sit up in bed and brushed her teeth and rinsed her mouth.

I hear these little footsteps moving fast and loud on the floor. I turned around, and it was our son running from the bathroom, all showered and dressed, running to his little sister's bed with a huge smile on his face. "Hi, sissy."

Our daughter was smiling at her little brother and said, "I'm fine. How are you?"

"I'm good too, sissy."

My husband and I were standing there with our arms around each other's waist, watching our beautiful children communicating with each other.

There was a knock on the door. My husband opened the door, and it was the nutritionist with a cart with food on it. She said, "Good morning, guys. How are you this morning?"

We all said, "Good morning, and we are good."

She said, "Great! I have your breakfast for you, and I will explain your daughter's menu to you, and then you can eat."

Our son asked, "Nutritionist, did you bring me the surprise the doctor said he had for me?"

She looked at our son, smiling, and said, "Yes, I did."

He said, "Oh, boy, thank you."

My husband said, "Let me help you in the dining chair so you can see what the doctor ordered for you." My husband sat our son in the dining room chair and pushed him up closer so he could reach his food and milk.

The nutritionist sat our son's plate in front of him on the dining room table, took the lid off his plate, and our son yelled, "Oh my god! Good ole pancakes—five of them!"

We all laughed.

My husband was cutting up our son's pancakes for him, and the nutritionist set up our daughter's meal for her on her bed table. My husband came back over to our daughter's bedside to hear what the nutritionist had to say about our daughter's meals. "Until your daughter is seen by the allergy specialist, her doctor wants us to eliminate eggs, cow milk, tree nuts, soy, peanuts, wheat, fish, shrimp, and other shellfish. When preparing her meals, check this list to make sure you are not giving her any of these foods."

Our daughter's breakfast was a dish of cantaloupe, one slice of bacon, a small bowl of cooked white rice with a cut-up banana in it (that is so nasty to me; I hope my baby will like it), a large glass of cranberry juice, and water. The nutritionist handed me a booklet and her office card with her name and phone number on it and said that we will have a better idea with our daughter's diet after we see the asthma specialist.

My husband and I thanked her. She said, "You're welcome. Bye."

My husband had three scrambled eggs, two toasts, four pieces of bacon, one slice of ham, grits, a glass of orange juice, and a cup of coffee. I had two scrambled eggs, two slices of toast with grape jelly, one small slice of ham, a glass of orange juice, a cup of coffee, and a large glass of water. Our son was really enjoying his breakfast, especially his pancakes; he loves pancakes. Our son also had a dish of cantaloupe, a glass of orange juice, a large glass of water, and one slice of bacon.

Our poor daughter wasn't enjoying her food as well, and I certainly could understand why. She didn't eat the white rice with the cut-up banana. She did eat her fruits and drink her juice and water.

Poor thing has to get used to a whole new food group now, but it is good for her health and well-being. With God's help, my husband, our son, and I will help her get well and live a good, healthy, long life.

After we had finished our breakfast, my husband put our son in the bed with his little sister so they could play for a while. My husband asked me if I would be okay with our children while he called his office! Of course, I said yes. My husband kissed my lips. He kissed our daughter and son on their foreheads and left the room. I was sitting there on the sofa in my daughter's hospital room, praying that our daughter would outgrow this asthma; she is a very active little girl, and I want her to enjoy her childhood as a normal child would.

There was a knock on the door. I got up from the sofa, went over to the door, opened it, and it was our daughter's doctor. "Good morning, beautiful family!"

The children and I said, "Good morning."

Our daughter's doctor had a smile on his face. He looked at my daughter and son and said, "Well, now this is what I like to see: you two playing together."

My son said, "Thank you, doctor, for my surprise pancakes."

The doctor and I laughed, and he told my son, "You're welcome. And how are you, little lady?" He was talking to my daughter.

She said, "I'm good."

"Wonderful! I am going to check your vitals, and if everything is as good or better than it was yesterday, I will do as I promised you, and that was to take all these things from you: your oxygen, heart monitor, IV, urinary catheter, and blood pressure cuff. Would you like that?"

My daughter said, "Yes, I would."

My daughter's hospital room door opened, and it was her dad. She had this huge smile on her face and said, "Hi, Daddy. My doctor is going to take all these things off me."

My husband, our daughter's dad, smiled and said, "That is wonderful news, baby girl. Daddy is so happy. I love you so much."

"I love you too, Daddy."

Our son asked his dad, "Do you love me so much too, Daddy?"

My husband picked our son up from our daughter's hospital bed and said, "Yes, of course, I love you very much, and your mom too."

Our daughter's doctor smiled and said, "You guys are a beautiful family."

My husband and I said, "Thank you."

The doctor called for his nurse's assistant to come to our daughter's hospital room. A few minutes later, there was a knock on the door. The doctor opened it, and it was his nurse's assistant. "Good morning, nurse."

"Good morning, doctor." The nurse looked at us and said, "Good morning."

We said good morning to her; she then looked at our daughter, smiling, and said, "Good morning, sweetheart."

Our daughter said, "Good morning."

While the doctor checked our daughter's vital signs, my husband, with our son on his lap and me sitting beside him on the sofa, watched the doctor and his nurse's assistant. Our daughter was watching everything her doctor was doing. After he had finished his examination of our daughter, he said, "Well, guys, everything is still looking good."

The nurse helped the doctor remove the IV, oxygen tube, heart monitor, blood pressure cuff, and the urinary catheter from our daughter. Our daughter's doctor said, "Okay, now we will see how your daughter does without these little guys." He was talking about the medical equipment he had on our daughter.

The doctor looked at his wristwatch and said, "I will be back to check on her in, oh, maybe four hours, but if you need me, I'm here. Hopefully, you won't need me."

My husband stood up from the sofa with our son, put our son on his left hip, took my left hand, and I stood up, and we thanked our daughter's doctor and nurse, and my husband said, "I hope we don't need to call you, doctor."

I said with confidence, "Doctor we will not have to call you or the Nurse, because everything will be fine." They smiled and said, "You're right. We will see you within four hours," and they left our daughter's hospital room.

My husband sat our son on our daughter's hospital bed beside his sister, fixed their bed pillows behind their little heads so they could watch TV together, and my husband lay down on the sofa where I was sitting, and he fell asleep.

I was watching our daughter to see how well she is doing without the oxygen, and so far, thank God she is doing great. I truly have the faith in God that He will continue to take care of our daughter for us and that she will live a long and healthy normal life.

I read in a book, I don't remember the book or who said it, but it said, "Faith sees through the storm." That statement has stuck with me to this day. I believe that believing is seeing, and I believe in God, and I am seeing how God is answering my prayers and healing our daughter.

I truly want to be clear to my readers that for me, it took seriously scary, painful things to happen in my life, a lot of praying, and for God to answer my prayers for me to develop my strong faith in God. I had to learn to call on God, depend on God, and trust in His words. I thanked Him every day of my life for His grace, mercy, and favors over my children and my husband.

My little family had fallen asleep, and I was close to going to sleep when there was a light knock on our daughter's room door. My husband immediately woke up and asked me if I was okay. "Yes, honey, it's the door."

He said, "Oh."

He got up from the sofa and opened the door; it was our lunch. I had ordered hamburgers and fries for lunch. The server sat our lunch on the dining room table. We thanked him; he said we were welcome and if there was anything else he could get us. My husband said, "No, thank you. We are good. Thank you."

He said, "Enjoy," and left the room.

My husband woke our son up, took him to the bathroom to pee, washed his hands and face, and brushed his teeth, and he did the same. I washed our daughter's hands and face, helped her brush her teeth and rinse her mouth with the mint mouthwash.

When my husband and our son came from the bathroom, our daughter said she needed to use the bathroom. I picked her up from her hospital bed; her dad came over and took her from my arms and took her to the bathroom for me and asked me to call him when our daughter was ready. Our daughter used the bathroom and washed her hands. I called out to my husband that our daughter was ready. My husband picked up our daughter and took her to her hospital bed.

I brushed my teeth, rinsed my mouth, washed my hands and face. When I came from the bathroom, our daughter asked her dad if she could sit at the dining table with us. "Yes, baby, of course you could." He got up from the table, picked up our daughter, and sat her in one of the dining chairs next to her brother.

I blessed our food and we ate our lunch. The hamburger, fries, and shake were delicious, and it was so nice to see my family at the table having lunch together.

After we had finished our lunch, the server came to get our dishes. When he opened the door, our son heard the children in the recreation room and wanted to go and play with them. Our son said, "Daddy, do you hear those kids playing?"

My husband and I laughed, and my husband said, "Yes, son, I heard the kids playing."

"Well, Dad, could I go play with them?"

"Well, son, let's go check with the nurse and see."

Our son was so happy; he asked his dad if sissy, his sister, could come too. "I think your sister needs to get her rest. Maybe tomorrow she could come."

Before my husband and our son left our daughter's hospital room, they both gave me and our daughter a kiss on our right cheeks.

When my husband asked the nurse in charge if our son could go to the recreation room to play with the children, she asked my husband if our son has had all of his immunization shots, and my husband said, "Yes, my wife makes sure our children get all of their shots on time."

The nurse said, "Great! Yes, you could take your son to the play area. How is your daughter doing?"

My husband said, "She is good, thank God."

I asked my daughter, "What would you like to do?"

She said, "Go for a ride in a wheelchair."

I got our daughter's wheelchair from the closet and put her in the chair, covering her legs with her special blanket. We stopped at the nurses' station to ask how far I could take my daughter for a wheelchair ride.

The nurse was so happy to see my daughter up in the wheelchair and not hooked up to medical equipment. The nurse said, "I am so happy to see you, little lady."

My daughter smiled at the nurse. I asked the nurse how far we could go, and she said, "Anywhere and for as long as you like. Just stay on this floor, and if you like, you could go to the recreation room."

I felt so good on the inside to see my daughter up and smiling and feeling up to playing and being around other children.

When we went into the playroom, our daughter was so happy to see her dad and brother and even more so to see the children. My husband was sitting at a table with four other men, talking. I guess they had sick children here in the hospital as well. Our son was playing with three other children, then he saw his sister, and he stood up and yelled, "Sissy, come over here!"

I wheeled her over to where her brother and his three friends were in her wheelchair. My husband came rushing over to me and our daughter and said, "Hi, baby, why didn't you have me paged? I would have come to you and our daughter."

I smiled at my husband and said, "Thanks, honey, but we went for a long ride in the wheelchair in the hospital. The nurse in charge said we would have to stay on this floor, and we did."

My husband picked our daughter up from the wheelchair and stood her on the ground. She gave her brother a hug and said she wanted to play with her friends. He said, "Okay, sissy."

His sister sat on the blanket with her two little girlfriends, and they played with different toys.

"Are you okay?" my husband asked.

"Yes, honey, I'm fine. Go back to your friends. Thanks for your concern."

"Okay." He went back to where his male friends were.

I looked over to the other side of the room, and I saw several women sitting at a table talking, and one of the ladies waved her right hand for me to come over. I smiled, went over, and introduced myself. The ladies introduced themselves to me. I sat down at the table with them. We talked and watched our children play.

The children were having so much fun, and that made me and the other parents so happy and thankful. I could hear all the talking and the laughter of the happy children while I was praying for God to heal *all* of those sweet little children.

Over the loudspeaker, a female voice said, "Okay, little ones, it's time for dinner."

Everybody said their goodbyes and went in different directions back to their children's hospital room. When my family and I got back to our daughter's hospital room, we had just enough time to get cleaned up before our dinner arrived. We all were happy and hungry.

For dinner tonight, we had fried chicken, mashed potatoes, cut green beans, candy yams, butter bread, cranberry juice for the children, and ice tea for my husband and me.

After our dinner and we were ready for bed, our daughter's doctor came to check on our daughter. He said, "I told you guys that I would check on your daughter within four hours to see how she was doing. I didn't come because I saw how well she was doing, and the nurses kept me posted at all times. I am so happy to see your daughter doing so well. She was a very sick child when she was brought into this hospital a few days ago."

Thank God for the healing. The doctor checked our daughter's vitals and said, "Things are still looking good. She is a bit tired, but that is understandable since she played so hard and for a long time today. That means she will sleep well tonight. I may discharge her from the hospital some time tomorrow if things stay the same or better.

"If you don't have any questions I will let you good people get to bed, and I'll see you tomorrow."

My husband said no, looking at me. I said, "I don't have any questions either. Thank you, doctor, and good night. See you tomorrow."

The doctor said, "You're welcome," and he left the room.

My husband and I said our prayers with our children, gave them a big hug, kissed them and told them we loved them more than anything, pulled the covers up over them, and lowered the night light.

The next morning when I woke up, I wasn't sure if I were dreaming or if what I was hearing was for real. I hear little voices laughing and talking. I opened my right eye and looked over toward our daughter's hospital bed, and there was our son in bed with his little sister, watching cartoons on the TV and talking like the characters in the cartoons.

My husband whispered in my right ear and said, "Good morning."

I said, "Good morning."

My husband and I said good morning to our children. They said, "Good morning, Mommy and Daddy."

We were looking at our children watching TV, and my husband said, "Isn't that a beautiful sight to see, our children having fun together?"

I said, "Yes, it is, and we better get up."

He laughed and said it was a good idea. My husband sat on the sofa, watching our children while I used the bathroom. I thanked God Almighty again for His loving blessing upon my daughter, my son, and husband.

There was a light knock on the bathroom door. "Yes?"

"Baby, it's me. I need to use the bathroom."

"Oh, honey, I'm so sorry. Please come in. I am finished."

When my husband came from the bathroom, he told our son that it was time for him to get showered and dressed before breakfast. The nurse's assistant came in to bathe and dress our daughter and change her bedding. My husband carried our son to the bathroom so they could get showered and dressed.

The nurse's assistant had finished bathing and dressing our daughter and had made her bed when my husband and our son came from the bathroom. The nurse's assistant asked if we needed anything else. I said, "No, but thank you." She said I was welcome and for us to have a good day. I said, "You have a great day too," and she left our daughter's room.

There was a knock on the room door, and our son said, "It is our food. I am ready to eat."

My husband and I laughed, and our daughter just looked at her brother with a beautiful smile on her face. My husband got up from the sofa and opened the door, and it was the server with our breakfast. Our son had wanted pancakes again, and our daughter wanted pancakes and bacon.

An hour after we had had our breakfast, our daughter's doctor came to her room. He said good morning to us, and we said good morning to him. He said our daughter's complexion looks good, and he would check her vitals, and if everything is stable, our daughter could go home today.

I was happy that our daughter slept well all night and without the oxygen. Her doctor said, "Her lungs, heart, and vital signs are good. She slept well last night without waking up, and her breathing was good, so, young lady"—the doctor was talking to our daughter—"you are good as gold. You can go home as soon as I sign your release papers, okay?"

Our daughter said, "Okay, doctor."

My husband and I said, "Thank you so much, doctor, for everything you have done for our daughter and us. We really appreciate it."

The doctor said, "You are more than welcome. You guys take care. And if you ever need me—I hope you will not—please call."

I said, "Thank you, doctor."

"Well, let me go sign your daughter's hospital release papers." He left our daughter's room.

My husband and I, our son, and our daughter were so happy that she is well, and we could go home. My husband helped our son pack his backpack. I packed our luggage. There was a knock on our daughter's room door. My husband opened it, and he had this surprised expression on his face. I asked, "Who is it, honey?"

My husband opened the room door wide, and standing in the entryway were several nurses and staff members with balloons, flowers, and two gift bags. I said, "Oh my god. Please come in."

They all came into our daughter's hospital room, smiling, and the nurse in charge said, "We are here to say bye to you all, especially this sweet little doll here"—she was talking about our daughter—"and this little handsome man"—she was talking about our son.

My husband said, "Thank you!"

Everyone laughed. Our son looked at his dad and said, "Dad, she was talking about me, not you."

We all laughed again, and the nurse in charge said, "Right, handsome man, I was talking about you. We have some balloons, flowers, a big card signed by the staff, and gifts for your beautiful children."

Tears were falling down my cheeks because my heart was so touched by the wonderful act of the hospital staff toward our children and us. Our children were so excited to see what all they had. I told them to wait until we get home. My husband, our children, and I thanked the hospital staff for everything.

The doctor came into our daughter's room with the hospital release papers for us to sign. My husband signed the papers, and our daughter's doctor said, "You are now released to leave this hospital."

The hospital staff that were in our daughter's room and her doctor gave us a hug and said, "Take care."

There was a light knock on our daughter's door; one of the staff members opened the door, and it was a staff member with a wheelchair for our daughter to ride downstairs to the hospital front entry. My husband said, "Oh, boy, I better go bring the car up."

The nurse in charge said she would wheel our daughter downstairs to the entry and make sure she is in the car safely. We all said and waved goodbye.

*****

It was another beautiful day. The sun was shining; the sky was a pretty midblue; the people were busy going from one place to another. I hadn't been outside since the day our sick daughter had been brought into the hospital. The fresh air and the warm heat from the sun felt good on my skin.

Our children played with their toys they had brought the day we had lunch with their father. My husband was quiet all the way home, and I was watching our daughter in the sun visor mirror, praying that she would not have another asthma attack. Then I thought about what I had heard my mom say to us many times: "Watch what comes out of your mouth. You could say bad things upon yourselves."

I said in my mind and heart, *God, please forgive me for thinking that. I know You have healed my daughter in Jesus's name. Amen.*

When we got home, our neighbors were standing outside in their driveways, waving at us and saying, "Welcome, neighbors."

We were smiling and said, "Thank you, neighbors."

Two of our male neighbors came over and helped carry our luggage and son inside our home. My husband carried our daughter. I yelled to our female neighbors that I would call them later. One of our female neighbors said, "Don't cook. We have your dinner ready for you. When you are ready, let us know."

I said, "Oh, thank you, guys. You are so sweet."

CHAPTER 6

I Was Not Happy to Hear What My Husband Had to Tell Me

My husband called me from his job and said he had to talk to me about something when he gets home. I could hear the hesitation in his voice. I took a deep breath. "Okay, honey, I will see you when you get home. Be safe."

"Okay, baby, I will," and we hung up our phones.

Four days later, my son and I were at my daughter's allergy specialist appointment. My children were playing with the other children in the playroom, waiting for the doctor to see my daughter. It was so hard for me holding back my tears and just yell and scream to the top of my lungs. I was confused and hurting and felt very betrayed. Because of what my husband told me four days ago. He said he had to go overseas and wouldn't be back in the States until they had completed their mission. I yelled and screamed at my husband, telling him that he had said he would be here for our daughter's appointment and for his family. He said, "I know I had, baby, but I don't have any control over this."

I said, "Yes, you do. Your commander knows your child is ill and that we need you here."

I remember that day so well. He packed his bags, went into the children's playroom, and told them he had to go away on his job, and he would be back soon. Our daughter jumped into her dad's lap with her around his neck, crying and saying, "No, Daddy. No, you can't go. Daddy, please. I love you."

He said, "I love you too, but I have to go to work, baby girl."

Our daughter jumped from her dad's lap and ran to me. I knelt down and held her in my arms, telling her, "It's okay. Your dad will be back home before you know it."

She cried and cried.

Our son stood there, looking at his dad for a few minutes, then he said, "Dad, why did you say you would be here with us and then change your mind?"

My husband picked up our son, sat him on his left knee, and said, "Son, I didn't change my mind. As I told your sister, it's my job, and I will be back before you realize I have been gone."

Our son said, "No, I won't," then he jumped from his dad's lap. "I love you, Dad."

His dad said, "I love you too, son."

Our son said, "No, you don't," and ran to his room.

My husband looked at me. I said, "Honey, go talk to him."

He said, "I have to go. I can't be late."

I said, "If you had told us sooner, maybe, just maybe, the children wouldn't react this way. They haven't before when you had to go out of the United States."

I picked up our daughter and went to my son's bedroom. My husband followed us. My son was crying and saying he hated his dad. I sat my daughter on my son's bed, put my arms around my son, and said, "Honey, no, you don't hate your dad. You are just upset right now, honey. He has to go to work."

My son didn't say anything else.

My daughter was no longer crying; she was watching her brother and me. I looked at my husband, and he said, "I am sorry."

My husband, my children's father, was just standing there, looking at us, then he walked over to us, kissed our daughter and son on their forehead, and said, "Bye, kids. I love you."

He asked me if I would come with him to the front door of our home. I looked at our children and said, "I will be right back."

They said, "Okay, Mommy."

I walked to the door with my husband, and I said, "I love you, honey. Take care of yourself. We will see you when you get back."

He kissed my forehead and said, "I love you too," then he picked up his bags and went out our front door.

This is why I am so messed up emotionally. I am very emotional right now because I didn't know what would happen to our marriage. I got my children ready, so we left for my daughter's doctor's appointment.

Three hours had gone by. My children and I were home, having our dinner. My daughter's allergy doctor had her medications and inhaler schedule set up, and everything went well with my daughter's appointment. After I got my children settled down, I tried to contact my husband to let him know how our daughter's appointment went and the medications she has to take, but I was not able to reach him.

Three weeks had come and gone and not one word from my husband. I called his commander, and he said that my husband and the crew were fine and that he would make sure that my husband gets my messages.

Every night for three months, I cried myself to sleep, missing my husband and not feeling too good on the inside of my stomach and heart, remembering how my husband let the children and me know that he was leaving us at the last minute.

I prayed every night for God to bring my husband, my children's father, home to us, but He didn't.

I asked God if this is the way it should be, then show me some kind of sign. Two days later, I noticed that my children were much happier, and I was surprised as to how my children never asked about their father or mention his name. Another thing, I noticed I had been sleeping well every night and couldn't remember the last time I cried for my husband.

I felt so bad for my children. It wasn't their fault that their dad had to go, and I felt bad for their father that his children acted as if they had forgotten about him.

Five months had come and gone, and my children and I had only talked to my husband, their dad, three times, and he said that he was still overseas and didn't know when he would be home. God was still taking care of me and my children. We were living a wonderful life.

CHAPTER 7

Too Many Heartbeats

The next morning, my son scared me almost to death. "Mom, Mom, come here. I can't open the bathroom door."

I ran down the hallway to my children's bathroom and pushed lightly on the bathroom door; there was something in the way. I squeezed into the bathroom, and—oh my god—there was my daughter there on the bathroom floor trying to catch her breath.

I got her asthma medication and her inhaler. I asked my son to get me a glass of water while I was helping my daughter use her inhaler. I was praying, "Oh, God, please don't take my child from me too."

My son handed me the glass of water, and my daughter took her medication. I called her doctor and told her what had happened, and she said for me to bring my daughter into the office.

My daughter's doctor told me after examining and talking to my daughter that something had upset my daughter. She didn't tell her doctor what or who upset her. My daughter's doctor said to me, "I don't know if I mentioned this to you. An asthma attack could be brought on by overexcitement, good or bad." The doctor left it at that. She said to continue to give my daughter her medication and get her injections twice a week plus use the inhaler, and she will see my daughter for a follow-up in three weeks.

I was wondering if my daughter was overexcited from talking to her father and hearing him say he didn't know when he would be home. I will talk with her when I think the time is right for her.

On our way home, my children were in the back seat of the car, playing, and I was giving thanks to God for taking care of my daughter again for me.

Nine months later, things are going good for my children and me, and I owe it all to God. We have a wonderful life, we are very close, we look out for each other, and I don't think of my husband as much. I try to talk to my children about him, but they would say, "Mom, it's okay. We don't want to talk about Dad."

CHAPTER 8

There Are Two Things We Could Say That Ring True

We could say what has happened in our lives, but we can't truly say what will happen in our lives. Ten and a half years later, my children and I are so happy. God has been very good to us, but something happened that I had to really call on God for His healing again. My faith in God was tested.

This was a beautiful morning. I was home alone. It was my day off work. After I had dropped my children off to school, I came home and cleaned my house. After I finished cleaning my house, I went into my bathroom to take a shower, and I got the scare of my life. While taking my shower, I did my monthly breast exam that my doctor had told me to do for years. I felt a small marble-sized lump in my right breast. I was terrified, I nearly fainted in my shower. I had to lean against my shower wall to keep from falling down.

No one wants to hear the word labeled the big C—cancer. The thoughts inside of my head were all over the place in my head. I do remember asking God to please let me live so I could take care of my children; no one would care for my children the way I would. I remember saying to myself that I would not let anybody know about the lump, not my mom, my family, or my doctor.

Let me say this to you, my dear readers: I really thought I was dying. Most of us think this way when we find a lump inside of our breast."

I remember John 16:24: "Until now have ye asked nothing in my name: ask, and ye shall receive, that your joy may be full." I realized that I had asked God to let me live, but I didn't ask in the name of His Son, Jesus Christ. I said, "God, please forgive me for not asking for Your help in the name of Jesus. I had asked God to forgive me because I didn't end my prayer request saying, "In the name of Jesus," when I asked Him to heal my right breast.

There was a calmness surrounding me. I felt different. I didn't know what had happened, but I remember hearing a voice clearly saying, "Are you able to drive yourself to my office?"

My God had led me to my telephone and made me call my doctor. I don't remember telling my doctor anything; all I know is that he said for me to come to his office, and I told my doctor that I would be there shortly.

I don't remember driving to my doctor's office, but there I was, sitting in my car in the doctor's office parking lot, and someone knocked on my car window. I looked, and it was my doctor's nurse. I looked up at the sky, the beautiful light-blue sky, and I said, "Thank You, God. Thank You."

The nurse opened my car door to assist me in getting out of my car. She put her right arm around my waist as we walked slowly into my doctor's office and back to the examination room. She gave me this gown to put on and said for me to tie the gown in the front and lie on the examining table. It was freezing cold in that room.

I put the gown on the way she said and got on the examining table. The nurse came in with a very warm blanket and laid it over me. The blanket felt so good to my cold body. The nurse asked if the blanket was warm enough, and I said, "Yes, it feels good."

She said the doctor would be right in, and she left the room.

I looked around the white room; everything was white, even the title on the floor, and the room was very cold. I was thinking about the lump I had felt in my right breast, and I started crying, and this scripture came to my mind: "Now faith is the substance [the lump in my breast] of things hoped for [God's will to heal my breast], the evidence of things not seen [my not knowing how God would heal my breast]" (Hebrews 11:1 NKJV).

There was a light knock on the door, and I said, "Come in."

The door opened, and it was my doctor and his nurse. My doctor said, "Hi, kiddo."

I said, "Hi, doctor."

He said, "Let me check the lump you found."

My doctor washed his hands and had me raise my left arm. He examined my armpit, then my left breast, then he had me raise my right arm, and he examined the armpit, then my right breast. He said, "Okay, my dear, this little thing keeps moving every time I try to catch it."

My eyes were huge, and I asked my doctor, "Is that bad?"

He said, "No. No, that is not bad. What I will do is draw some fluid out and send it to the lab."

I asked him "Would you do it with me awake?"

He said, "Yes, but I will numb the area so you won't feel anything."

I said okay. My doctor told the nurse to let him know when we were ready, and he left the room. The nurse said, "Everything would be fine, sweetie." Then she wheeled this table over to the examining table where I was lying on with lots of different types of items on a stainless steel tray.

She put a white dressing cloth under my right breast, cleaned my whole right breast with something cold, then she inserted that needle into my right breast to numb it some more before my doctor drew the fluid out. The nurse asked me how I was feeling. I said, "Okay."

She said, "Great," then she left the room, and in a few seconds, there she was and my doctor.

My doctor said, "Okay, let's get started."

The nurse assisted him with putting on his rubber gloves. I had my eyes closed very tightly and prayed for God to not let me feel any pain. The nurse held my left hand while my doctor inserted the large needle into my right breast, drawing out the fluid. I was so scared, I turned to the doctor and nurse. The next thing I remember is my doctor saying, "Okay, young lady, all done." He put a Band-Aid on the area. "I will give you something for the pain. I don't want you to worry about anything because everything is fine. God is in control."

Wow, this was the first time I had heard my doctor say God's name. That made me feel much better to hear him say that along with me still having my faith in my God.

"Okay, there will be a small amount of bleeding. That's normal. There will be some swelling. That's normal. You can use an ice pack for fifteen minutes then heat for twenty minutes off as much as needed. I want to see you back here in a week for a follow-up, okay?"

I said, "Okay, doctor. Thank you."

He said, "You are welcome, and no worries." He left the examining room.

The nurse helped me sit up and fixed my blouse. The nurse said she would walk me out to my car and for me to call the office and let them know I made it home safely. I said I would.

As I was driving away from my doctor's office parking lot, I looked at my car clock and saw that I had more than enough time before I had to pick my children up from school. I was grateful that I had put the children's dinner in the oven earlier because as soon as we get home and they wash their hands, they will be ready to eat dinner.

Oh my god, speaking of eating—with me feeling that lump in my right breast and coming to my doctor—I forgot I had left our dinner cooking in the oven. I have to rush home. I was praying that our home didn't catch on fire.

As soon as I said that, I heard the fire truck, and it passed me, going in the same direction I was going. I really started praying. Then the fire truck turned on my street. I said, "Oh, God, don't let the fire be too bad." I didn't see any smoke, and that made me feel a little better.

When I turned on my street, I didn't see any smoke—no fire and no fire truck. I said, "Oh, God, thank You so much."

I parked my car, and when I got to my front door, I leaned toward the door to see if I could smell smoke, but I couldn't, so I unlocked the door and walked inside, and everything was fine. I thanked God again for taking care of everything for me. I went into my kitchen; the burners were on low heat; the oven was on 250 degrees instead of the normal 350 degrees. I sat down on one of my sofas and cried like a baby, not because I was in any pain but because of how good God is to me.

One might say that I turned the burners on low and that I lowered the temperature on the oven to 250 degrees through all of the excitement of finding that lump in my right breast! Maybe I don't remember anything about burners and ovens; all I remember is talking to my doctor and him telling me to come to his office right then. Anyway, whether I did it or my guiding angels, I am thankful that all is well. There are these scriptures in the Bible:

> So Jesus said to them, "But because of your unbelief; for assuredly, I say to you, if you have faith as a mustard seed, you will say to this mountain, move from here to there, and it will move; and nothing is will be impossible for you." (Matthew 17:20 NKJV)

> For all the promises of God in Him are Yes, and in Him Amen. (2 Corinthians 1:20)

I remembered what God did for my older daughter ten years ago, saving her life when she had a severe asthma attack and was hospitalized for four days. She still has asthma, but given God the glory, she is doing very well with her asthma shots twice a week, taking her asthma medications, and eating the right foods and drinks. He healed my daughter. I know He will heal my breast and that there is no cancer. I am standing on His promise to me.

I went into the kitchen to check on dinner. Everything was good; nothing was burned up. I still had some time before I had to pick up my children from school, so I called my supervisor at my job to let her know about the lump I found in my right breast and that I had gone to my doctor and what happened.

The telephone at my job rang and rang. It must be very busy at the hospital because the phone doesn't ring this many times before someone answers it. Finally, a familiar voice came on the phone. "Hello, Mt. Odessa Hospital. This is Nurse Hartor speaking. How may I help you?"

I said hello to my favorite supervisor. Nurse Hartor laughed and said, "I'm good, and I am your only supervisor. Why are you calling this hospital on your day off?"

"I am calling you because there is something I have to share with you."

"I don't like the sound in your voice. Is there something wrong with my godchildren?"

"Oh, no, the children are fine. It's about me."

"Okay, what about you?"

"When I was taking my shower this morning, I did my regular breast self-exam, and I felt a small marble-sized lump in my right breast."

"Oh my god, how are you?"

"I'm okay."

"Okay, did you call your doctor?"

"Yes, my angel did it for me."

"Okay, who was your angel?"

"My guardian angel called my doctor for me."

"Okay, great. What did your doctor say and do?"

"Well, he examined my breasts, numbed the areas on my right breast where I felt the lump, removed some fluid from my breast, sent it to the lab, and said he would call me as soon as he got the result from the lab. He told me not to worry. Everything would be fine and that God is in control of everything. I am to see him again in one week for him to check my breast and make sure there are no more lumps."

"Did he remove the fluid in his office?"

"Yes, he did, and, boy, you should have seen that huge needle. Why am I saying this to you? You are a nurse. You have seen and used huge needles before."

"Okay, is there anything you need me to do for my godchildren or you."

"No, everything is under control. Thank you. Get back to work. I will keep you posted."

"Okay. Take care. Bye."

"Bye."

Okay, now that I have gotten that out of the way, I will take my pain medication, and check the Band-Aid area. Everything looks good, so I am going to take a nap before I have to pick my children up from school.

I wasn't sure if what I was dreaming was real. I heard dogs barking. Finally, I was fully awake. I looked at the clock on the dining room wall and was happy the barking dogs woke me. It was close to the time to pick up my children from school. I looked out of my family room window and saw why the dogs were barking. The postman was new, and the dogs had to get acquainted with him. I wonder if our regular postman is on vacation.

Once I arrived at my children's school, I realized I had some time to get myself together so that the children wouldn't feel any concerned feelings coming from me. A few minutes later, I see my daughters coming to their waiting spot.

It is impossible for my son to be waiting with his sisters at the spot where I pick them up after school is out. Watch when my son gets into the SUV, he will have a great reason as to why he was unable to be here on time, waiting with the girls. The girls are always here at the waiting spot, not my son. The girls got into the SUV. "Hi, Mom. How was your day off?"

I wonder how my children would feel if they knew what type of day I had. I told the girls I had a great day. "How about your day?"

My younger daughter had to tell her sister and I that she had a not-so-good day because one of her friends didn't come to school today because she is sick. My younger daughter said, "I am not finished. I did all of my school homework at school."

My older daughter asked her little sister, "Are you finished with telling us about your day?"

She said, "I am."

I said, "Honey, I am so proud of you, and I am so sorry that your friend is sick. Hopefully, she will be better tomorrow.

She said, "Thanks, Mom."

My older daughter told her little sister that she was proud of her finishing her schoolwork and that she was sorry to hear that one of her friends was sick. I don't know why, but my younger daughter laughed and said, "Thank you, sissy."

"Would you believe that your brother is still not here?"

My younger daughter said, "Leave him, Mom. I bet tomorrow he would be here waiting on you."

My older daughter and I laughed, and my older daughter said, "Mom, I agree to leave him."

I said, "Girls, come on now. You wouldn't want me to leave you, would you?"

They both said no. My younger daughter said, "Mom, here comes your slow son."

We laughed.

As my son approached the SUV, I could see the fear in his eyes. "Hi, mom. I am sorry I am late. The coach had something to tell us. Oh, Mom, could you give my friend a ride home?"

"Where does your friend live?"

"Stan, this is my mom."

"Hi, Mrs. Barron."

"Hi, Stan."

"These are my sisters."

"Hi, sisters."

The girls laughed and said, "Hi, Stan."

My son said, "Mom, I will show you where Stan lives."

I said okay. My son got inside of the SUV in the front seat, and Stan got in the back with my girls. My son told me which way to turn to get to Stan's home.

When I dropped Stan off at home, he said, "Thank you, Mrs. Barron. Bye," and told my son he would call him later.

We made it home, and as soon as my son opened the front door, we could smell the aroma of the food I had prepared for our dinner. I turned off the house alarm. My children went to their rooms to put away their backpacks and went to their bathrooms to wash up for dinner.

My children talked as they ate their dinner. I was listening to them, but at the same time, I was thinking about the morning I had concerning the lump I had discovered inside of my right breast and going through the ordeal of my doctor's drawing the fluid from my right breast with that huge needle. I love my children so much, and I knew that God would make sure that my breast wasn't cancerous because my children needed me, and I needed them.

I heard my son say, "Mom, are you okay?"

I looked at my son and said, "Yes, son, why do you ask?"

He said, "Because we said thank you for the delicious dinner, and you didn't answer, just looking down at the dining table."

I said, "I am sorry, guys. I was just thinking about how much I love you guys."

My children looked at each other, then looked at me, and my older daughter asked, "Mom, is there anything wrong?"

I looked at them, smiled, and said, "No, honey, there's nothing wrong."

My younger daughter said, "Mom, are you sure?"

"Yes, baby, I am sure, and I am glad you guys enjoyed your dinner. Thank you."

My children got up from the dining table and came over to me and gave me a hug and kiss and said they love me more and that they would clean the kitchen and dining room. I said, "Thank you, guys. I will go into the family room and put up my feet."

I tried not to keep looking at the phone, wondering if my doctor would call me with the results of my lab test, and if he did, how would I react in front of my children? I looked at the wall clock on the dining room wall. It was 5:45 p.m. My doctor's office is closed now. I am going to relax and let my faith in God take control.

My son came into the family room to tell me that he had finished his school homework, and he would get a shower. I was so happy to hear him say he did his school homework because my son likes to wait until the last minute to do things.

I could hear my daughters talking as they were on their way to their bathroom to get their showers. I was wondering what time my doctor would call me tomorrow. I hoped it would be after I had taken my children to school.

I went to my bedroom, got my shower, checked my breasts, and I could still feel the small marble-sized lump inside of my right breast. I took a deep breath and examined my left breast. Everything was fine. I checked my right breast, everything except for the soreness and pain, my right breast was fine, thank God.

After I had gotten in my bed, there was a light knock on my bedroom door. I said, "Come in."

It was my three beautiful children coming to say they love me and good night. I love my children so much. "I love you guys too. Good night. I will see you in the morning."

CHAPTER 9

Waiting Anxiously

Wow, the next morning came so fast to me. I looked at my clock on my nightstand; it was 6:30 a.m. I could hear the children in their bathrooms, getting their showers and getting ready for school.

After I had showered, dressed, got my purse and car keys, and gone into the family room, my children were waiting for me. I dropped my children off at school, told them that I love them, for them to be safe, and I would see them that evening when they get out of school. They said, "We love you too, Mom, and you be safe. We will see you after school is out."

I hurried home, hoping my doctor would call me about the results of the fluid he drew from my right breast. When I got inside of my home, I looked at the answering machine to see if anyone had called.

I sat down in my recliner chair and started reciting Psalm 23:1 (KJV):

> The Lord is my shepherd; and I shall not want.
> He maketh me lie down in green pastures: he lea-
> deth me beside the still waters. He restoreth my

soul: he leadeth me in the paths of righteousness for his name's sake. Yea, though I walk through the valley of the shadow of death, I will fear no evil: for thou art with e; thy rod and thy staff they comfort me. Thou preparest a table before me in the presence of mine enemies: thou anointest my head with oil; my cup runneth over. Surely goodness and mercy shall follow me all the days of my life: and I will dwell in the house of the Lord for ever.

I believe that reading in the book of Psalm 23 covers every area of my life. My dear readers, would you take time and read the Psalm 23? I mean, really read it.

My house phone rang. I took a deep breath, then I answered my phone. "Hello."

The voice on the other end of my phone was my doctor. He said, "Good morning."

I said, "Good morning, doctor."

He said, "I am calling you because I just got your lab test results back, and"—my heart was beating so loud inside of my chest to me—"I have good news."

My heart started relaxing some.

"There are no signs of any malignancy in the fluid. However, I would feel much better if I remove the lump from your breast and have it tested as well. That way, we both could relax, okay?"

I was praying to God, thanking Him for the healing and hearing my doctor saying he would like it if I could come into his office this morning so he could remove the lump. I said, "Thank you so much, doctor, for getting back to me with the great news, and, yes, I could come to your office right now."

My doctor said, "Great, see you soon. Goodbye."

I hung up my house phone and thanked my God again for His wonderful blessing, not letting the fluid from my right breast be cancerous.

I don't remember driving to my doctor's office. I was too anxious about the procedure my doctor was going to do to my right breast. I was wondering if he would do it in the hospital, and if so, how long would I have to stay in the hospital? I don't want my children and family to know about this, plus I have to pick my children up from school on time.

When I went into my doctor's office, his nurse was waiting for me. She said, "Good morning, sweetie."

I said, "Good morning."

She took my left arm, and I followed her to one of the examining rooms. I took a deep breath and said in my low voice to the nurse, "This is the same examining room I was in yesterday. This is a good omen."

The nurse said, "Yes, it is. This is why I brought you back to this examining room."

The nurse gave me a clean white gown to put on and said for me to have the gown opening in the front and that she would be right back. I got on the white sheet on the hard examining table. The examining room was so cold. I wanted to get up and put my clothes back on. The room was all white, freezing cold.

Just as I was getting ready to get up and get my clothes, there was a light knock on the door, and the door opened. It was the nurse with two heated blankets she put over me. My god, those heated blankets felt so wonderful to my freezing body. I said, "Nurse, you are right on time. I thought I was going to freeze to death in here. This room is so cold."

The nurse said, "I am so sorry, sweetie. I should have had these heated blankets already ready for you. How are you feeling now? Are you warming up?"

I said, "Oh, yes, I feel much better now. Thank you for the heated blankets."

There was a knock on the door, and the nurse opened the door. It was my doctor, wearing all white—white pants and white doctor's jacket. He said good morning again. I said, "Good morning, doctor."

I asked my doctor if he would be doing my surgery in the hospital. He said, "No, I will do it right here."

I asked, "Would I be awake when you do the surgery?"

He chuckled and said, "Yes, you would be awake."

My heart hurts with fear pains. I said, "Oh, doctor, I can't do this."

He said, "Yes, you can because I will give you a local anesthetic, and I will numb the site surrounding the lump."

I noticed while my doctor and I were talking, his nurse wheeled a stainless steel cart close to the sterile table I was on with different types of medical instruments on it. I said, "Okay, doctor, I am ready."

My doctor's nurse said, "Okay, doctor, are you ready?"

My doctor said, "Yes, we are ready."

My doctor's nurse assisted him by putting on his sterile rubber gloves. I closed my eyes and started praying to God to guide my doctor's hands as he removed this lump from my right breast.

My doctor's nurse held my left hand while my doctor did his job of localizing the site surrounding the lump in my right breast and then started his procedure of removing the lump. To me, it seemed like my doctor was taking hours to remove the lump. I didn't feel any pain or discomfort; it's just that he had told me, that it would only take thirty to forty-five minutes to take the lump out.

I was sweating now, not from the heat of the blankets—they felt good—but from fear. My inner spirit said to me, "Where is your faith?"

I relaxed and said inside of my head, *Thank God for bringing me back to my healer—You, God.*

My doctor said, "Okay, dear, all finished."

I opened my eyes, and I couldn't believe what I saw. My doctor was standing there with a jar in his right hand, and in some type of fluid, there was this thing floating in the fluid inside of the jar that appears to have several long legs attached to it. The thing looked like an octopus. I asked my doctor where he got that thing in that jar from. He said, "This is the lump that was inside of your right breast, and as you can see, I didn't cut any of the branches. I got the whole thing."

I said, "Oh my god, how could this be? The lump I felt inside of my right breast felt the size of a small marble."

My doctor said, "This thing [the lump] was deep into your breast tissue. That's why it took me longer than I had anticipated, and as I said, I got the whole thing from its roots. Everything looks good from my view, but we will know for sure when we get the lab results back."

My doctor's nurse called down to the lab and asked if someone would come and get my mass for a biopsy test. My doctor said, "This is what I need you to do: stay calm, use your right arm less as possible, take your pain medication on time because as I told you, I had to go deep into your breast tissue, so you will be in great pain if you don't take the pain medication on time.

"Do not get the dressing on your right breast wet. If the dressing gets too bloody, you can change it. Now if there appears to be too much bleeding, you contact me immediately.

"And you need to call your job and let them know that you will be off work for at least two weeks. I still want you to come in next week. I will contact you as soon as I receive your biopsy result, and again, don't worry. God got this one too, okay?"

I said, "Okay, doctor, I will do everything you have instructed me to do. Thank you, doctor."

My doctor said that I was welcome and for me to take care; he would be in touch with me soon. My doctor's nurse helped me sit up on the examining table and helped me get dressed and down off the examining table.

Since I didn't want my children to notice me using my right arm differently, I decided we would have fast food for dinner tonight, and I would cook tomorrow evening's dinner while they were at school. *What am I thinking? Today is Friday. We always eat junk food over the weekend. Thank God, it's Friday.*

When I got home, I parked my SUV in my car garage, hoping that would make people think I wasn't home. The medication had me a bit sleepy. I needed to take a nap anyway. But first, I needed to call my job and give my supervisor the update on my medical situation and that I would be off work for at least two weeks.

I told my supervisor about the surgery my doctor did on my right breast right in his office. I described to her how the lump looked that my doctor took out of my right breast. When I said the lump looked like an octopus with several long legs attached to it, she said, "It looked like a what?"

She asked me, "Were you scared when you saw it?"

I said, "Yes, I was scared. That thing was not what I was expecting to see. Well, I won't hold you any longer. I just wanted to give you an update and time for you to get someone to cover my shift."

My supervisor said to me, "Don't worry about work. You take care of yourself. Do you need me to come down and help you with my godchildren?"

"Oh, no, thank you. If you came down during the week, the children would be asking questions, and I don't want that."

"Are you trying to confuse me? Today is Friday, the beginning of the weekend."

"Oh, that's right. I am sorry."

"No worries. I understand you have been through a lot these past few days. Okay, but if you need my help while the children are in school, let me know."

I laughed and said, "Thank you, friend. I will, but remember, today is Friday. It is almost time to take my pain medication, and I need a nap before I pick up the children."

"Okay, I will check on you later this evening."

"Okay, thanks."

I had taken my pain medication and got comfortable on the sofa facing the family room picture window. I was saying to myself, *I wish I had thought about it and asked my doctor to take a picture of that lump—that octopus-looking thing—for me so I could show it to my friend/supervisor.*

When I picked up my children from school, I asked them if they would like to have their favorite fast food for dinner tonight. My younger daughter said, "We would love to, Mom."

My son and older daughter said, "That sounds good to me."

We asked how everybody's day went, and everybody said the day was good. I could tell that my children's minds were on what they wanted to get for their dinner. I had to drive to three different food places for my children to get what they wanted for dinner, but that's okay because I love my children and that God had let me live and be able to do this for my children.

Once we got inside our home, my children ran to their bathrooms to wash up so they could eat their food. We enjoyed our dinner while we talked. The children said they did their school homework during the study period at school.

My children cleaned up the kitchen. My son said he was tired and was going to get his shower and go to bed. I said, "Okay, son. I love you."

He kissed my right cheek and said he loved me, good night, and he would see me tomorrow morning. He said good night to his sisters. They said good night to him, looked at me, and said, "Thanks for the dinner, Mom. I love you. Good night. See you tomorrow morning."

I said, "You're welcome. I love you too. See you tomorrow morning."

We hugged each other, and the girls went to their rooms.

After my son had gotten his shower, he yelled, "Thanks for the dinner, Mom."

I yelled back, "You're welcome, son. Good night."

I checked to make sure all the doors and windows were locked and the house alarm went to my bedroom. I took a bath instead of a shower; this way, I won't get the dressing wet on my right breast, where my doctor did the biopsy.

After my bath, I took my pain medication. I am pretty tired myself. Hopefully, I will sleep well tonight. And I hope my children and their friends who are staying the night keep down the noise.

I was in my bed and comfortable when my phone rang. I answered my phone, and it was my supervisor. She said, "Hi, I was checking on you before you fell asleep. How are you?"

I said, "I am good. I had my bath, and I just took my pain medication. I think I will sleep well tonight. I am pretty tired."

My supervisor said, "You should be tired. You have been through a lot these past two days. I want to wish you good night. I will call you tomorrow. Okay, good night."

I said my prayers, giving thanks to God for goodness, mercy, and healing. I remember it as if it was yesterday when I was thanking God for the life and health of my older daughter when she was hospitalized for serious asthma attacks when she was five years old.

I thank God that she has been doing really well. Now here I am, trusting in God and thanking Him for taking care of my health.

CHAPTER 10

Everything Will Be Alright

I had a dream last night that my deceased father was standing at my bedside looking at me. He looked so well and still young; he had on a brown suit. I truly believe that that was a confirmation from God that everything is well with my right breast. "The prophet who has a dream, let him tell a dream" (Jeremiah 23:28).

The house phone rang. I thought one of the children would answer it, but they didn't. I haven't been to the bathroom yet, and I haven't had my coffee. I don't need to talk to anybody. Then I thought about my doctor. I picked up the phone receiver in my bedroom on my nightstand and said hello. The voice on the other end of my phone was my doctor. I was not expecting to hear from him over the weekend. He said, "Hello. Are you still there?"

I said, "Yes, doctor, I am here how are you?"

"I am well. Thank you for asking. I told you that I would call you when I got the results back from your biopsy. I couldn't let you go the whole weekend worrying.

"I have fantastic news for you, my dear! Your little octopus, as you call it, is benign. In other words, there are no signs of malignancy."

I burst out crying, saying, "Thank You, God. Thank you, doctor. I knew when I dreamed about my deceased father visiting me last night that that was God's confirmation for me that He had taken care of my right breast."

"I will agree with you, my dear. God has all kinds of ways of letting His children know beforehand that He has answered their prayers. Since everything is good and you are not having any problems with your breast, I will let your breast heal, and I will see you in two weeks. How does that sound to you?"

"Oh, doctor, everything sounds good to me. Thank you again, doctor, and you have a great weekend."

"You're welcome, enjoy your weekend too."

I said, "I sure would, doctor. Goodbye."

And my doctor said, "Goodbye, dear."

I remembered the passage in the Bible.

> And Jesus answering said unto them, Have faith in God. For verily I say unto you, That whosoever shall say unto this mountain [the lump that was inside of my right breast], Be thou removed, and be cast into the sea; and shall not doubt in his heart, but shall believe that those things which he saith shall come to pass; he shall have whatsoever he saith. Therefore I say unto you, what things soever ye desire, when ye pray, believe that ye receive them, and ye shall have them. (Mark 11:22–24)

Lord knows my desire was for God to remove any and all illness from my body and cast them into the deep sea.

I have to continue to read these scriptures to help increase my faith in God, and when God helps me get through difficult times, my faith in Him gets stronger and stronger. My God, He healed my older daughter, my faith in how He helped my children and I get through the ordeal of losing my husband, my children's father, and now, healed my right breast.

I do believe that my husband loved me and our children, and that he knew we loved him too. It has been over ten years now, and God has helped keep my children and me well and with a good life. The lump that was inside of my right breast, the outcome of it has truly increased my faith in my God.

I would like to ask you—my readers, my audience, my brothers and sisters in Christ—to read Mark 11:22–24. Read it over and over until you get it into your mind, heart, and soul. God loves us.

> For God so loved the world, that he gave his only begotten Son, that whosoever believeth in him should not perish, but have everlasting life. (John 3:16 KJV)

> For God sent not his Son into the world to condemn the world; but that the world through him might be saved. (John 16:17)

I come that they might have life, and that they might have it more abundantly. (John 10:10b KJV)

I called my friend to tell her the wonderful news I had gotten from my doctor concerning the lab results from my biopsy. I heard this deep voice on the other end of the phone say hello. I said, "I am sorry. I must have dialed the wrong number."

The deep voice said, "Oh, no, wait. You have the right number, girlfriend, but please tell me why are you up so early. This is the weekend."

I said, "I am so sorry. I didn't pay any attention to the time. I was so excited. I will call you back later. No, you call me when you are up."

My friend said, "You better not hang up your phone. I am sorry. Did you hear from your doctor? What did he say?"

I said, "Take a deep breath, sis. I am fine, and, yes, I did hear from my doctor, and everything is fine, no signs of cancer, and I am to see him in two weeks for a follow-up on the healing of my right breast where he did the surgery."

My friend screamed so loud, saying, "Thank You, Jesus. Thank You, God. I knew everything would be fine because I know how much faith you have in God."

"Thank you, sis. I knew for sure that everything would be fine because I dreamed that my deceased father visited me last night. He looked so well and young. He had on a brown suit."

"I can't wait to get to work Monday so I can let the staff and patients know that you are well and good. You know they all love you so much."

"I know they do. I just loved all the flowers, cards, candies, and great books they sent to me."

"I love them as well. Look here, girl. We have to go out to dinner tonight and celebrate God's love, healing, and great mercy for you. Let me treat you to dinner, okay?"

"Hey, sounds great to me."

"Okay, you can pick the restaurant."

"Okay, great. I will be at your house at 7:30 p.m."

"Okay, I will see you at 7:30 p.m. Bye."

I got my Bible from my nightstand drawer and turned to Hebrews 4:16. I knew the book, chapter, and what verse, but I didn't remember the verse exactly. "Let us therefore come boldly unto the throne of grace that we may obtain mercy, and find grace to help in time of need" (Hebrews 4:16).

I am so happy that I have this great relationship with God. When I need God's help with something in my life, I go to Him boldly and make my request be known.

Oh, please let me say this to you: God does *not* love me or my children any more than He loves you and your family. How do I know this to be true? "For there is no respecter of persons with God" (Romans 2:11).

CHAPTER 11

Thank God That Happy Days Are Here Again

I went to my bathroom and took my bath without getting my dressing on my right breast wet, brushed my teeth, rinsed my mouth, and went downstairs to take my pain medication and have my coffee. I am so excited about what God has done for me. I am hungry. I will cook breakfast for the children and myself. I don't know how many children are here, but given how good God has been to me, making that lump (tumor) that was inside of my right breast be benign, I would cook breakfast for all of the children on my block.

I cooked smoother white potatoes with onions, garlic, salt, mushrooms, butter, and American cheese. I cooked some bacon, eggs, grits, and I toasted toast. I put jelly, milk, orange juice, cranberry juice, and butter on the dining room table.

I could hear the children laughing and talking, saying who would get the bathrooms first and how good the aroma of my food smelled and how hungry they were. I laughed to myself. I love it when my children enjoy my cooking.

My two daughters came downstairs to the dining room before the boys. They said, "Good morning, Mom."

"Give me a hug and kiss on my right cheek."

Their girlfriends said, "Good morning."

I was so happy that my girls didn't hug me tight on my right breast.

When my son and his friends came downstairs to the dining room, my son came over to me, kissed my right cheek, and hugged me very tightly, but he didn't come near my right breast. "Good morning, Mom."

I said, "Good morning, son."

My son's friends said good morning to me and the girls. My son and his friends said, "Boy, your food sure does smell delicious."

I said, "Thank you, guys, and if someone would bless the food we could eat."

After we finished our breakfast, the children said they would clean the kitchen and the dining room. I went to my bedroom, changed my bedding, started the washer, cleaned my bathroom, and I felt the pain in my right breast. I looked at the clock on my nightstand, and it was ten minutes past the time I should have taken my pain medication.

The pain was so painful. I wondered if I would be able to go to dinner tonight. I called the house phone downstairs. My older daughter answered the phone, and I said, "Honey, would you bring me a hot cup of water?"

"Sure, Mom."

There was a light knock on my bedroom door. I said, "Come in."

I looked at my bedroom door and was surprised to see all of the children coming into my bedroom with concerned expressions on their faces. I asked, "What is wrong?"

My son said, "That's what we want to know, Mom."

I looked at all of the children standing there, waiting for an answer from me. I said, "There is nothing wrong. Why do you guys think there is something wrong?"

My smart little younger daughter said, "Mom, you only drink hot water when you take a pill for your headache."

I laughed and said, "Oh, you are so smart, right? I do have a light headache. I will be fine."

The concerned expression on their faces disappeared, and I was so happy. I didn't know what the children knew. I am so glad my younger daughter said what she said. That helped me a lot with an excuse. God, please forgive me for not being honest with my children.

My son said, "Do you need anything else, Mom?"

"No, sweetie, I am fine—really."

My older daughter handed me my cup of hot water. I sat it on my bedside nightstand and said, "Hey, guys, don't make me feel sad. I am fine. I was going to tell you guys that your godmother and I are going out to dinner tonight."

"Oh, okay, that sounds good, and we are sorry, Mom. We don't want you to feel sad. We were just concerned about you."

"I know you were, son, and it's okay. I am pleased that you guys care about me."

My older daughter said, "We not only care about you, Mom, we love you," and they all came over to my bed to give me hugs. I made sure that I protected my right breast.

I said, "Now that you guys know that I am fine, would you please go do whatever it was that you were doing before I asked for a cup of hot water?"

The children left my bedroom. I took my pain pill and got under the covers.

When I woke up, it was time for me to take another pain pill. I went to my bathroom, brushed my teeth, rinsed my mouth, and went downstairs while the children were watching TV. They looked up at me and said, "Hi, Mom. Did you sleep okay?"

"Hi, guys. Yes, I did."

My younger daughter asked me, "Mom, did your headache leave?"

I smiled and said, "Yes, sweetie."

My children asked me if they could go to their friend's house for a few hours. I said, "Sure, but I need you guys home before your godmother and I leave for dinner."

My son said, "We would be back home long before you leave."

I said, "Okay, you guys, be safe."

There was a car horn honking. My son said, "Bye. That's my friend's mom."

Shortly after my son and his friends had left, the front doorbell rang. My youngest daughter said, "I got the door. It's my friend's auntie. Bye, Mom."

"Bye, baby. Be safe."

An hour later, my older daughter said, "Okay, Mom, our ride is here. I will see you later."

"Okay, sweetie. Be safe."

I sat in home mode on the house alarm and went to my bedroom, looking in my clothes closet to find something to wear to dinner tonight. I laid my clothes and everything out that I would wear tonight, took my pain medication, and got in my bed so I could take a nap before going out to dinner tonight.

I heard the house alarm beep. It must be my children. "Hey, Mom, could we have pizza for dinner tonight?"

"Yes, son."

"Thanks, Mom."

I got out of my bed, remade it again, went into my bathroom, and ran my hot bathwater. There was a knock on my bedroom door. "Yes! Come in."

It was my two daughters. "Hi, Mom, we just wanted to let you know that we were home."

"Good. Did you girls enjoy yourselves?"

"Yes, we did. What time would Godmother be here?"

"She said she would be here around 7:30 p.m."

My girls went downstairs when they heard the front doorbell. I could hear voices saying, "Hi, Godmom, it's so good to see you."

Then I heard my two daughters scream, "Oh my god, hi, Mom!"

I went downstairs, and there stood my supervisor, friend, my children's godmother. I said, "Hey, girl."

She said, "Don't I have the sweetest children in the world?"

I laughed and said, "Yes, you do."

My friend asked me if I knew what restaurant we would eat at. "Yes, how about Chinese food?"

She said, "That sounds good to me. Are you ready?"

"Yes, I am."

I told my children the dos and don'ts. My friend and I gave the children a kiss and hug. I told my children that I would see them in about two or three hours.

Whenever I got into my friend's car, she asked me how I was feeling. I feel good that I have taken my pain medication. My friend said, "Congratulations on your wonderful news about your breast biopsy not being cancerous. I didn't want to ask you how you were feeling in front of the children."

"Thank you for remembering not to say anything in front of them. They gave me a slight scare earlier today when I asked my daughter—number 1—to bring me a hot cup of water—"

My friend interrupted me and said, "The only time you drink hot water is when you are taking pain medication."

I said, "Exactly! That's when my daughter—number 2—said, 'Mom, you only drink hot water when you are taking a pill for a headache.'

"There they all are, standing there, waiting to hear my answer. I laughed and said, 'You are so smart. I do have a light headache, but I will be fine.'"

"Ooh, wee, sis, God is going to get you for lying."

"No, God won't. I asked Him to forgive me immediately after I said it. I know He didn't like me lying, but He knew why I did."

"Okay, sis, that's between you and God."

"Yes, it is. Thank you."

After my supervisor and I had finished our dinner, I thanked her for being a good friend, and I told her about my scare with my right breast and asked if she would share my story with her staff at the hospital's next staff meeting.

Everyone who reads my book, listen to me. It does *not* matter what your race, religion, ethnicity, etc. may be. We are *all* God's children, and He loves us equally.

Your life and health *matters*. *Early detection matters*. If you notice anything—I mean, anything—unusual with your body, see your doctor; pray and ask God to take care of the situation for you. Trying faith is a wonderful thing. If you read my book's entirety, you understand what I meant by "trying faith is wonderful."

Remember to read Mark 11:22–24 as many times as you have to.

> And Jesus answering saith unto them, Have faith in God. For verily I say unto you, That whosoever shall say unto this mountain [whatever it is in your life that you need God to fix], Be thou removed, and be thou cast into the sea; and shall not doubt in his heart, but shall believe that those things which he saith shall come to pass; he shall have whatsoever he saith. Therefore I say unto you, What things soever ye desire, when ye pray, believe that ye receive them, and ye shall have them.

Again, my dear readers, I have to pray and read God's scriptures all the time to keep me focused on God and increase my "faith" in God. I am so happy that I tried faith. May God continue blessing *all* of you!

ABOUT THE AUTHOR

Irene Horn-Brown was born in a small town named England, Arkansas. Some frightening things happened in Irene's life, and she believed that in order to survive those things, she had to have a relationship with God and have faith in God.

CPSIA information can be obtained
at www.ICGtesting.com
Printed in the USA
LVHW111228160422
715982LV00018B/57